GAY AND LESBIAN WRITERS

Sappho

GAY AND LESBIAN WRITERS

Sappho

Jane McIntosh Snyder
and
Camille-Yvette Welsch

Lesléa Newman
Series Editor

CHELSEA HOUSE
PUBLISHERS
A Haights Cross Communications Company ®

Philadelphia

CHELSEA HOUSE PUBLISHERS

VP, NEW PRODUCT DEVELOPMENT Sally Cheney
DIRECTOR OF PRODUCTION Kim Shinners
CREATIVE MANAGER Takeshi Takahashi
MANUFACTURING MANAGER Diann Grasse

Staff for SAPPHO

EXECUTIVE EDITOR: Matt Uhler
EDITORIAL ASSISTANT: Sarah Sharpless
PHOTO EDITOR: Sarah Bloom
SERIES AND COVER DESIGNER: Takeshi Takahashi
LAYOUT: EJB Publishing Services

A Haights Cross Communications ⬧ Company ®

http://www.chelseahouse.com

First Printing

9 8 7 6 5 4 3 2 1

Library of Congress Cataloging-in-Publication Data
Snyder, Jane McIntosh.
  Sappho / Jane McIntosh Snyder and Camille-Yvette Welsch.
    p. cm. — (Gay and lesbian writers)
  Includes index.
  ISBN 0-7910-8220-2
  1. Sappho. 2. Poets, Greek—Biography. 3. Lesbians—Greece—Biography.
4. Women and literature—Greece—History—To 500. 5. Lesbos Island
(Greece)—Biography. I. Welsch, Camille-Yvette. II. Title. III. Series.
  PA4409.S65 2005
  884'.01—dc22
                              2005005508

Cover: © Getty Images, Inc.

TABLE OF CONTENTS

PRIDE

MANY YEARS AGO, IN 1970 to be exact, I began my career as a high school student. Those were the dark ages, before cell phones and CD players, before computers and cable TV, before the words "gay" and "pride" ever—at least to my knowledge—appeared in the same sentence. In fact, I remember the very first time I saw the word "gay" appear in a newspaper. It was in the early 1970s, a year after the 1969 Stonewall riots when a group of butches and drag queens fought back against a police raid on a gay bar, sparking what was then known as the "gay liberation movement." I was sitting in our Long Island living room with my brothers, my parents, and some visiting relatives. One of the adults picked up the newspaper, read a headline about the anniversary of Stonewall and said in a voice dripping with disapproval, "Well, all I can say is *gay* certainly meant something different in my time." There were a few murmurs of agreement, and then the matter was dropped. I learned very quickly that this subject was taboo in the Newman household.

Not that I had any inkling that I would grow up to be a lesbian. All I knew was that I didn't want to get married and have children, I wasn't interested in boys, and all I wanted to do was read books, write poetry, and spend time with my best friend, Vicki, who lived three houses away. My friendship with Vicki was strictly platonic, but even so, taunts of "Leslie the lezzie, Leslie the lezzie" followed me up and down the hallways of

Jericho High School. (I changed my name from Leslie to Lesléa when I was sixteen largely because, due to my gender-free name, I was, much to my horror, enrolled in the boys' gym class.)

Interestingly enough, Vicki was never once teased for being a lesbian; did my classmates know something I didn't know?

In 1973 I left home to attend the University of Vermont. There was no gay/straight alliance on campus, nor were there courses in gay literature or gay history. Though I studied the poetry of Gertrude Stein, I was never led to believe that Alice B. Toklas was anything more than the poet's housekeeper and cook. Though I studied Walt Whitman's work and read the novels of James Baldwin, there was never any mention of either man's sexuality. And even though I still was unaware of my own sexuality, I knew somehow that I was "different." I did not want the same things most of the young women around me wanted, namely a husband and children. I did not know being a lesbian was a possibility. Since I wasn't interested in boys "that way," I simply thought I was not a sexual being.

What saved me was the Beat movement, and specifically the Beat poets: Allen Ginsberg, Peter Orlovsky, Gary Snyder, Anne Waldman, and Ted Berrigan, all of whom became my teachers when I hitchhiked out to Boulder, Colorado, and enrolled in Naropa Institute's Jack Kerouac School of Disembodied Poetics. The Beats were unabashedly sexual. Allen and Peter were clearly a couple; there was also a pair of lesbians on the faculty who made no secret of the fact that they lived together. I learned about Sappho and the island of Lesbos; I learned that Virginia Woolf and Vita Sackville-West were not merely pen pals; I learned that Emily Dickinson had a correspondence with her sister-in-law Susan Huntington Dickinson that some interpreted as romantic. And though these women may or may not have been lesbians, the discovery that women could be primary in each other's lives in a passionate way filled me with a sense of excitement and hope. Finally I realized that I wasn't a freak. There were others like me. A world of possibilities opened up before my eyes.

In 1999, I was invited back to my alma mater to be inducted into the Jericho High School Hall of Fame. The world had changed in many ways since I graduated in 1973. The words "gay" and "lesbian" now appeared in many newspapers across the country on a regular basis, and the gay, lesbian, bisexual, and transgendered community even had its own newspapers and magazines. In 1977, Harvey Milk, the first openly out politician in this country, had been elected as a San Francisco City Supervisor (tragically he was assasinated in his office the following year). Most large cities had gay and lesbian pride parades during the month of June and many high schools had gay straight alliances (Concord High School in Concord, Massachusetts started the first GSA in 1989). The "gayby boom" had begun as more and more lesbians and gay men were starting families, and the gay marriage movement was going strong.

Since graduating from high school, my life had changed dramatically as well. In 1988 I met the woman of my dreams and a year later, on September 10, 1989, we celebrated our relationship with a lifetime commitment ceremony (On September 10, 2004, we renewed our vows before a justice of the peace, making our fifteen-year marriage legal in the state of Massachusetts). I had published close to thirty books, most of which had gay or lesbian content, including the picture book, *Heather Has Two Mommies*, which became one of the most controversial and challenged books of the 1990s. And I had become a political activist, speaking out for the rights of lesbians and gay men every chance I could.

When I was inducted into Jericho High School's Hall of Fame, I was invited to come to campus to give a speech at a school assembly. It was only upon arrival that I was informed that the students knew only one thing about me: I was an author. They did not know the titles of my books and they did not know I was a lesbian. Consequently, I had the unexpected opportunity to come out to an entire high school population. If the students were surprised, they did not show it. Jericho students are nothing if not polite. But they did ask interesting questions. They wanted to know if I had dated boys when I was in high school (yes); they wanted to know how old I was when I came out (twenty-seven); they wanted to know if I wished that I were straight (no, but sometimes I wish my hair was). At one point the questions came to a halt, so I decided to ask my audience, "What is it like for gay and lesbian students today at Jericho High School?" The auditorium was quiet for a moment and then a boy called out, "We don't have any gay students."

About a year later, I received an email from a Jericho High School alumna who graduated in June of 1999. She told me she was a lesbian and had known so since she was fifteen years old. She had been at my induction assembly, but did not feel comfortable coming out in front of her peers that day, or even privately to me. Only after she graduated from high school and went away to college did she feel safe enough to be out. Clearly many things had changed since I'd attended Jericho High School and many things had not.

A book is a powerful thing, and literature can change people's lives. If I had read a biography about a lesbian writer when I was in high school, I truly believe my life would have been vastly different. I might very well have been spared years of pain and confusion because I would have known that a life very much like the one I am now living is possible. If the books in this series had been on the Jericho High School curriculum in 1999, perhaps the young woman who sent me an email would have felt safe enough to come out of the closet before graduation.

It is my hope that this book and others like it will help high school students know that not everyone is heterosexual, and that gay, lesbian, bisexual, and transgendered people can and do live happy, productive, inspiring, and creative lives. The writers included in this series have certainly left their mark on society with their award-winning works of poetry and prose. May they inspire us all to be exactly who we are with pride and celebration.

—Lesléa Newman, 2004

SAPPHO, LYRICIST OF LESBOS

There was a time, in the early 1980s, when almost every lesbian I knew had a dog or a cat named Sappho. I once met a donkey who carried the name. In my adopted hometown of Northampton, Massachusetts during this time, a lesbian feminist bookstore called Womonfyre proudly displayed the book *Sappho Was A Right-On Woman* in the window. An a cappella group called the Sapphonics performed on a regular basis. Their specialty was parody and I remember a very funny song called "There Is Nothing Like a Dyke" sung to the tune of "There Is Nothing Like a Dame," from the Broadway musical, "South Pacific."

Before I sat down to read Jane McIntosh Snyder's fine biography of Sappho, I decided to search out poetry written by poets who were inspired by the woman Plato referred to as "the tenth muse." It did not take me long to find several poems in collections on my bookshelf that mention Sappho by name. In a poem entitled, "Invocation to Sappho," Elsa Gidlow asks, "Sappho, all roses, / do we not touch / across the censorious years?" Rita Mae Brown begins the poem, "Sappho's Response" with the line "My voice rings down through thousands of ages ..." and ends with the wonderful call to arms: "An army of lovers shall not fail." Robin Morgan ends a poem entitled "Lesbian Poem" with these provocative lines: "So get off my back, Sappho. / I never liked that position / anyway." And Eileen Myles published a book of poetry called *Sappho's Boat*, though the poet's name is not mentioned in any of the individual poems that appear in the collection.

Next I decided to read poetry written in a form called "Sapphics," which I first studied when I was a student of Allen Ginsberg's at Naropa Institute. Allen explained that Sapphic verse was named for the poet Sappho who lived on the island of Lesbos in the period around 600 B.C.

A Sapphic stanza consists of four lines. The first three lines are usually eleven syllables long and the fourth line is usually five syllables long. It is believed that many of Sappho's songs were written in this form, and many contemporary poets use the form to this very day. Poets who have written Sapphic verse include Marilyn Hacker, Annie Finch, Ezra Pound, Louise Bogan, William Meredith, and James Wright.

As I read, I kept reminding myself that Sappho lived 2,600 years ago. Imagine someone 2,600 years from now (the year would be 4605) writing a poem that mentioned you by name, or that you inspired! It's pretty hard to wrap one's mind around such a concept. What will the world be like so far into the future? Will people be reading and writing poetry? Will people be reading and writing at all? What would Sappho say if she knew that her work outlived her by thousands of years? What would she say if she knew that the very mention of her name implies women who love women? Case in point: the book *The Girls: Sappho Goes to Hollywood* written by Diana McLellan is a study of many of Hollywood's greatest stars including Greta Garbo, Marlene Dietrich, Tallulah Bankhead, and the women who loved them.

And if all that wasn't enough, Sappho even appears in *Webster's Encyclopedic Unabridged Dictionary*. The definition next to her name reads: "Greek poetess born in Lesbos." Directly above her name appears the word "sapphism" which comes from Sapph(o) + ism. The definition of "sapphism" reads simply, "lesbianism." There is an irony to this, as the concept of identifying oneself according to one's sexual preference did not exist at the time of Sappho's life.

Many lesbians hold the island of Lesbos in their minds as a mythical Paradise where beautiful women in loose flowing gowns stroll by the sea, playing lyres and singing love songs to each other. How closely this dream resembles Sappho's actual life is something we will never know. Only one of Sappho's poems, commonly referred to as "Hymn to Aphrodite" exists in its entirety. The rest of her work is known to us only in fragments, some as short as a single word. And it is from these bits and pieces that scholars for centuries have tried to piece together the story of her life.

I find the story of Sappho's poems and how they have been preserved through the ages equally as fascinating as the story of Sappho herself. As Jane McIntosh Snyder tells us, some of the poems were passed down orally and then eventually written down on parchment made of animal skins. Other poems, or more accurately fragments of poems, were found on scraps of papyrus (made from fibers of an Egyptian plant) and tucked into mummy wrappings. These have only been discovered in the last one-hundred years. Lastly, at least one poetry fragment was found scratched onto a piece of broken pottery.

The question that is posed most often regarding Sappho is: was she or was she not a lesbian? In a way, the question is irrelevant, since the concept of "lesbianism" did not exist during her lifetime. The real question, then is, did Sappho have romantic feelings for other women? I believe the answer is a resounding *yes*. The proof is not only in her own work, but in the fact that her work has been censored at various times throughout history. For example, in the poem "Hymn to Aphrodite," the original

Greek clearly shows that the narrator of the poem and the object of the narrator's affection are both female. Yet there have been translations where the narrator's longed-for-love is portrayed as male. If the poem was merely about female friendship, there would be no need to censor it, or to use Jane McIntosh Snyder's word, "de-lesbianize" it.

What Sappho's poems tell me is that women who fall in love with other women have been around for a long, long time. And undoubtedly we will continue to be around for a long, long time. With any luck, we will still exist 2,600 years from now. And if that's the case, I'm sure that we, along with other lovers of literature, will still be reading and discussing Sappho's poetry with admiration and awe.

one

Was Sappho a Lesbian?

What did Sappho of Lesbos teach girls, except how to love?'

—Ovid, (Tristia 2. 365)

SAPPHO, ONE OF THE GREATEST WRITERS of songs in ancient Greece, lived in the period around 600 B.C. on the large green Aegean island called, then as now, Lesbos. Indeed, it is from the name of her homeland, located in the Aegean Sea just a few miles off the coast of what is now Turkey, that the modern term *lesbian* derives, for many of her songs speak about passionate love between women. Unfortunately, only one song has survived to the present day in its entirety, but there are enough fragments of several other songs that she wrote to give us a reasonably good idea of her themes and subject matter. Who knows, perhaps someday the wrappings of a mummy excavated in Egypt may yield more papyrus rolls that will include some of Sappho's poetry. Many pieces of Greek literature have been preserved for us in this way, for the mummies of the Hellenistic period were often buried with their favorite reading material for the afterlife.

Even on the basis of what little survives of Sappho's songs, most readers at the end of the 20th century would agree that her words portray erotic love between women. When the female narrator of one song describes her reaction upon seeing another woman with words such as "the instant I look upon you, I cannot anymore/speak one word,/But in silence my tongue is broken, a fine/fire at once runs under my skin,/with my eyes I see not one thing" (see chapter 5), there seems little doubt that Sappho is speaking of what we would today call—hearkening back to Sappho's homeland—"lesbian" love. Yet as you will see as you read this book, Sappho's lesbianism has often been minimized or even erased altogether.

THE ISLAND OF LESBOS

What do we know today about the island on which Sappho lived and composed? It is the third largest island in the Aegean Sea (665 square miles) and lies so close to the Turkish mainland (ancient Lydia) that you can easily see it from the eastern shores of the island. In ancient times people traveled by small boat, usually island-hopping as much as possible rather than striking out into the middle of the Aegean Sea. Today most people visiting Lesbos go by jet from Athens, the modern capital of Greece. The trip takes only a little more than half an hour. Visitors usually include Athenians who were raised on the island and are going home to visit relatives, as well as a healthy sprinkling of people from northern European countries such as England and Germany. For them, Lesbos is what Florida is for Americans—a pleasant, warm place to escape for a week's vacation.

Lesbos, whose population today is a little under 100,000, is a beautiful island that has fortunately been spared the severe deforestation suffered by some of the Greek islands. One of the most fertile areas in all of Greece, it is rich in olive trees and vineyards. As in ancient times, life on the island is primarily rural, although today there is some manufacturing in the form of textile mills and soap-making factories. The climate is generally moderate, with cool summers and mild winters. The people in the small villages are quite friendly towards strangers. When I visited Lesbos in the 1980s, I traveled for the most part by public bus and on foot and had many occasions to talk with the local people (in my pidgin modern Greek, no doubt mixed with bits of ancient Greek) to get help with directions. I was offered, and accepted, everything from delicious large oranges to a donkey ride up a steep hill to visit an old Genoese castle from medieval times. When the villagers learned that I was an American, they invariably produced a postcard from a cousin or a niece who lived in Chicago or New York.

One of the purposes of my trip to Lesbos was to visit the town where Sappho was born. According to ancient legend about the poet (to which we shall return in more detail in the next chapter), she was from the town of Eressos on the southwest coast of the island. After arriving at the airport at what is today the only real city on the island, Mytilene, I was met by a small van from the hotel I had booked at Methymna, on the north coast, where I wanted to begin my visit. The driver turned out to have just returned to his homeland after 15 years of working in Australia, so he spoke English fluently and offered the passengers a guided tour en route. The scenery on the drive to the north was beautiful—sea, mountains, pine trees, olive trees, all sorts of greenery, fields of bright red poppies, and many sheep and goats. The clear air felt wonderful, especially after spending several days in Athens, where the atmosphere is often heavily polluted. We soon arrived at the hotel in Methymna, home of another famous singer in ancient times named Arion. Today we know little about him except for a charming story reported by the ancient Greek historian Herodotus (*Histories* 1.23–24). He tells how Arion, about to be robbed and murdered at sea, stood up on deck singing and playing his lyre, with the result that a dolphin came to his rescue and transported him safely back to dry land, where he was later able to confront the mutineers.

For a couple of days I explored Arion's homeland and other scenic spots along the north coast, the region that was famous in ancient times for its fine wine. I then set out on a winding bus journey through the mountains and small villages of the island's interior, and after many triple hairpin turns and much honking of horns, arrived in what is known today as Skala Eressou. Skala Eressou is the site of the ancient town of Eressos, of which a few scattered ruins remain on a steep hill (acropolis) overlooking a small harbor and the modern village. (Today Skala Eressou functions as a summer town for the people of modern Eressos, a small town a couple of miles inland; in winter, everyone moves back to the inland town.)

Appropriately, the village's tiny inn was called the Hotel Sappho, and the town square was named after Sappho as well. Most of the visible ruins on the acropolis are from many centuries after Sappho's time, from the Roman and Byzantine periods, but there are traces of polygonal stone walls that may date from as early as the 7th century B.C.

After exploring the area near Skala Eressou, including the nearby petrified forest at Sigri—its trees are preserved in volcanic ash from some 700,000 years ago—it seemed to me that perhaps Sappho was not so remote in time from the present day as I had first thought. Resting in my room one evening at the Hotel Sappho after a tasty dinner of *dolma* (stuffed grape leaves) and *tsipoura* (a local fish) prepared by the proprietor's wife, I listened to the sound of the sea lapping at the sandy beach not far from my window, and thought that if one just imagined away a few cars and Mercedes buses and other modern conveniences, one could almost see Lesbos through the eyes of Sappho nearly 2,600 years ago.

We know from archaeological evidence, from remarks in Sappho's poetry, and from comments in the poetry of her male contemporary, Alcaeus, that in ancient times this green and fertile island had close commercial and cultural ties to the nearby mainland (Lydia). The island is only six miles away from the mainland at its closest point, so such interchange is not at all surprising. In addition, Lesbos's many natural harbors made trade and communication with neighboring peoples relatively easy. Archaeological research on Lesbos has not been as extensive as it has in some of the more famous areas of Greece (such as Athens, Olympia, or Delphi), but the discoveries made so far indicate that the island was an important center of Greek culture at least from the time of the Bronze Age many centuries before Sappho. Indeed, the name of Arion's town, Methymna, has been shown to be of pre-Greek origin, probably a holdover from the days before the island was occupied by Greek-speaking people.

Certainly there was a well-established tradition of lyric poetry on Lesbos, that is, poetry meant to be sung to the accompaniment of a lyre. In addition to Sappho and Alcaeus and the legendary singer Arion, 7th-century Lesbos was also the birthplace of another famous musician named Terpander, about whom little is known today. The island's proximity to the mainland no doubt resulted in a rich exchange of cultural influences that would not likely have occurred in the case of a more remote island. Looking back over the island's history, perhaps we could say that the 7th century B.C.—Sappho's time—was its cultural heyday. In later days the island did produce two other important writers, the historian Hellanicus (ca. 496–ca. 411 B.C.) and the philosopher Theophrastus (ca. 370–ca. 288 B.C.), who eventually became the head of the school founded in Athens by Aristotle, the Lyceum. The muses seem to have continued to inspire writers from the island even in modern times, for one of Greece's Nobel Prize winners, the poet Odysseus Elytis, is a native of Lesbos.

WAS SAPPHO A LESBIAN?

The most obvious answer to this question is "Of course! After all, she lived on Lesbos!" However, what is usually meant by the question in modern discussions of Greek literature is more along the lines of "Was she a homosexual?" In answering such a question, we need to remember that the terms used in English today to indicate a person's sexual orientation (homosexual, heterosexual, lesbian, gay, etc.) are modern terms that have only been in use for a little over a hundred years. Although to judge from their art and literature the ancient Greeks were certainly well acquainted with erotic love between members of the same gender, particularly males, they used no such labels to classify individuals. What we would call homosexual behavior was not frowned upon per se. In fact, in ancient Athens a homosexual relationship between a teenage boy and a mature man was generally regarded as a positive phase of the younger partner's educational and social development; such a relationship was not expected to prevent his eventual marriage and fatherhood. What was frowned upon in sexual relationships between men was passivity. It should be stressed, however, that among the ancient Greeks there was no underlying moral, religious, or social basis for censuring the erotic relationships between males that conformed to the expected hierarchical arrangement involving an adult male and an adolescent boy. Indeed, such relationships are celebrated both in their philosophical literature (in the various dialogues of Plato) and in their lyric poetry (particularly the poems of Anacreon of Teos).

As for relationships between females, we have much less information, since much Greek art and literature tends to be androcentric, that is, centered on men. The majority of Greek literature was written by men, who generally considered the activities of males of far greater interest and importance than those of females (see chapter 3). The important point to note, however, is that the Greeks evidently did not subscribe to the same categories of sexual classification that are in use today. Our present-day terms, after all, are only modern constructions based on modern ways of looking at the world, not timeless truths that will necessarily be valid in the future. Indeed, our current understanding of gender is much more complex than the old binary system of "male" versus "female." Children are now classified by the medical community as (1) female, (2) male, (3) hermaphroditic (sharing the characteristics of female and male), (4) male becoming female (through hormonal treatment and/or surgery), and (5) female becoming male. It may be that at some time in the future, an equally complex scheme for designating sexual orientation will come into use. It is all really a question of the human imagination!

When we look at the question "Was Sappho a lesbian?" from the viewpoint of the ancient Greeks, then, we can see that such a query might have been unintelligible to them, since they did not categorize people on the basis of same-gender or opposite-gender sexual orientation. Indeed, the English word *lesbian* did not take on its modern meaning—a woman whose primary emotional and sexual bonds are with other women—until the late 19th century, when it appeared in a medical dictionary of 1890. (The medical context reflects the disease model of homosexuality that still permeates some contemporary discussions of the subject.) The term *lesbianism* appeared slightly earlier, in 1870 (see the multivolume *Oxford English Dictionary* for details).

If we were to ask the question differently, however, and inquire whether Sappho's songs included pieces about one woman's erotic love for another, the answer would certainly have to be yes. Sappho wrote many kinds of songs, most likely for use at many different kinds of occasions: weddings, public religious festivals, private ceremonies, parties of various sorts, and religious rituals. Among the songs that seem most likely to have been intended for occasions of a private sort (whether religious or secular) are several fragments that are clearly centered on a female narrator's erotic feelings for another woman. As we will see in the next chapter, although Sappho's poetry was widely admired in ancient times for its beauty, readers of her poetry in the 19th and 20th centuries have often been uncomfortable with the direct expression of erotic passion between women. As a result, they have sometimes gone to great lengths to explain away what we would refer to in our modern terminology as the lesbian aspects of her songs. In this book, then, I will use *Lesbian* (with an uppercase *L*) to refer simply to the island of Lesbos; I will use *lesbian* (with a lowercase *l*) to refer to erotic and/or emotional love between women. As the fragments of Sappho's poetry suggest (see chapters 4, 5, and 6), there is little doubt that Sappho was both a Lesbian and a lesbian.

chapter

two

Sappho's Life and Reputation:
A Partial Reconstruction

Some say there are nine Muses: how careless!
Behold, Sappho of Lesbos is the tenth!

—Plato

UNLIKE THE MODERN FIGURES CONSIDERED in this series, about whom there is generally an abundance of information in the form of letters and diaries written by them and their friends, reviews of their work, legal documents, and so forth, Sappho is known to us primarily through sources of a much later date than her own lifetime in the 7th and 6th centuries B.C. Many of these sources are of dubious reliability, for ancient biographers of famous writers often tended to accept as fact what we would label as legend. They were particularly fond of fantastic death stories, in which some famous person dies by leaping into a volcano, for example, or jumping off a cliff into the sea.

Unfortunately for us, in our curiosity about important figures of the ancient past, we have very little information about Sappho that can be considered true. Besides their penchant for the legendary, ancient biographers also tended to invent "facts" on the basis of an author's writings, treating their words as though they were autobiographical statements rather than literary fictions. (We have to remember that if a poet begins a poem with a line like "It was Friday the Thirteenth, and on the way to the laundromat I ..." ... such a statement may have little or no bearing on what actually did happen to the author that day.) Despite all these problems with the ancient sources, in the sections below I will try to distinguish the few credible biographical details about Sappho from the more obviously legendary elements. Because there is so little that can be certainly known about Sappho, each era has tended to construct its own ideas about what sort of life she led, for whom she wrote her songs, how she fit into the social or religious structures of ancient Lesbos, and so forth. These later constructions have been highly influential in the interpretation of Sappho's songs, so we shall look at some of them as well in the final section of this chapter.

A VERY SHORT BIOGRAPHY OF SAPPHO

Sappho was born toward the end of the 7th century B.C. during the time usually referred to as the archaic period of Greek history. As we saw in chapter 1, her birthplace was the town of Eressos on the southwest coast of Lesbos. Her name, which she herself mentions in several of her poems, would have actually been pronounced "Psappho." Since this is a difficult cluster of consonants for speakers of English to pronounce, we usually just follow the Roman adaptation of her name and call her Sappho.

As for her family, who lived in Mytilene, her father's name was Skamandronymos and her mother's name was Kleis. Evidently she had three brothers: Erigyios, about whom we have no information; Charaxos, who made business trips to Egypt and is mentioned by Herodotus in his *Histories*; and Larichos, who served on the governmental council of Mytilene. It was a time of great political turmoil on the island, especially among rival aristocratic factions struggling for control of Mytilene after the overthrow of the royal family. Despite her brother's political involvement, Sappho herself seems to have been rather uninterested in the machinations of the rival groups, for she only once refers to one of them in the remaining fragments of her songs (frag. 98b Voight). In order for her brother to have served on the council, he would have to have been a member of the aristocracy, so we can conclude that Sappho was from an aristocratic family.

Our ancient sources also report that Sappho was married to a man named Kerkylas, who came from the island of Andros, one of the Cyclades islands in the middle of the Aegean Sea. She may also have had a daughter, named after her own mother (Kleis), who seems to be mentioned in two of the fragments of her songs. The husband is sometimes assumed by modern scholars to be fictitious—especially by those who cannot reconcile the idea of Sappho-as-wife with Sappho-as-lesbian. A more feasible objection is that Kerkylas may be a made-up name, for scholars have noticed that it bears a suspicious resemblance to a Greek word for penis, *kerkos*; in combination with the name of the presumed husband's birthplace, Andros, which suggests the Greek word for man, we may be dealing with a comic allusion to "Dicky-Boy from the Isle of Man" that somehow worked its way into the biographical tradition.

One final detail emerges from the ancient sources, and that is a report of Sappho's temporary refuge on the faraway island of Sicily (off the "toe" of Italy) during a time of particularly great political unrest at Mytilene. Such a trip certainly seems credible, given what we know of frequent travel on the part of the ancient Lesbians and the extremely bitter factional strife at Mytilene alluded to in the poetry of Alcaeus, Sappho's contemporary.

The poet Alcaeus is in fact the one contemporary source that we have about Sappho—that is, a source who was alive and writing roughly when she was. Alcaeus, who lived in Mytilene, seems to have alluded to her by name in one of his songs (unfortunately, the Greek text of the original poem is not entirely clear): "O weaver of violets, holy, sweet-smiling Sappho ..." (frag. 384 V.). Although we do not have the rest of the song, we can guess that Alcaeus is complimenting Sappho on her divine talents as a poet. The allusion to weaving violets may in fact be a metaphorical reference to the making of song, for weaving imagery in Greek literature is frequently used to describe the creative process of composing poetry. We have some 400 bits and pieces of Alcaeus's songs left today, but he never mentions Sappho in any of the other remaining fragments.

SAPPHO IN ANCIENT LEGEND

The most dramatic tale about Sappho, which seems to have originated some two centuries after her death, has to do with a lover's leap off the White Rocks of Leukas. Here, off the west coast of mainland Greece, there are steep cliffs, from which Sappho was supposed to have jumped off into the sea out of desperate love for a handsome man named Phaon. Aside from the obvious motif of a dramatic death story (common, as I noted earlier, among ancient biographies of poets and other famous people), another reason for us to be skeptical of this tale involves the appearance of this same Phaon in other, clearly mythological contexts. According to Greek myth, even Aphrodite herself (the goddess of love, also known to us by her Roman name, Venus) was supposed to have fallen in love with Phaon. Later she hid him in a bed of lettuce so that no rival could find him and take him away from her. In addition, there are other ancient legends about people jumping off the White Rocks of Leukas, including one where Aphrodite leaps off the cliffs out of love for a young man called Adonis.

Although the earliest version of the Sappho–Phaon story occurs in a fragment of a comedy by Menander in the 4th century B.C., the most influential account of Sappho's death leap was not written until the early part of the 1st century A.D. The authorship is not entirely certain, but it is thought that the famous Roman poet Ovid wrote a poem in the form of a letter (*Heroides* 15) that purports to be the words of Sappho (in Latin, of course). In the letter, "Sappho" describes her love-making with Phaon in explicit detail and bids farewell to her lover. This poem, published along with other letters attributed to other ancient heroines (Dido, Medea, Penelope, etc.), was enormously influential in perpetuating the legend of Sappho's unhappy death, however unlikely such a tale may have been. Given the obvious mythological and metaphoric implications of the story, it is likely that if Sappho ever did refer in her songs to leaping off the White Rocks of Leukas, she meant the phrase in a nonliteral way, perhaps as a metaphor for falling into a swoon. Eventually, it may be that later writers interpreted the phrase (if indeed she used it) as referring to a literal leap, thus giving rise to the suicide legend.

Other details that emerge from the pseudobiographical material available to us include a clearly unreliable report of Sappho's physical characteristics. According to a papyrus from Egypt dated to the early 3rd century A.D. (some 900 years after Sappho's death!), she was short, dark-complexioned, and ugly. Today we in fact have absolutely no way of knowing what she may have looked like, for the four labeled representations of her on vases were all painted at least a hundred years after her lifetime, and none of them bears any particular resemblance to the others. Unlike political and literary figures of the 5th and 4th centuries B.C. (such as Pericles and Plato) who were represented in sculptures executed during their lifetime and that have survived (at least in Roman copies) to this day, Sappho had no luck in being visually immortalized. The Roman orator and politician Cicero reports that there was a fine bronze statue of her made in the 4th century B.C. by Silanion. He says that the statue (which of course may have borne no resemblance to what Sappho actually looked like, since it was executed two centuries after she lived) stood in the town hall of Syracuse, Sicily, until it was stolen for personal enjoyment by a corrupt Roman governor of the 1st century B.C. At any rate, no identifiable statues of Sappho have survived the passage of time. We do, however, have a few coins that were minted on the island of Lesbos up through the 3rd century A.D. that bear Sappho's portrait and an identifying label, but these representations are quite small and very likely give us no idea of what Sappho really looked like.

SAPPHO'S LATER REPUTATION

For several centuries following her death, Sappho seems to have enjoyed great fame as the author of songs known for their beauty and power of expression. Plato even dubbed her "the tenth Muse" (the usual mythological catalog includes only nine Muses—Calliope, Clio, Euterpe, Thalia, Melpomene, Terpsichore, Erato, Polyhymnia, and Urania, each of whom was thought to inspire different kinds of literary and artistic undertakings). A story is told of the great Athenian statesman Solon (late 6th century B.C.), who as an old man was supposed to have been especially captivated by one of Sappho's songs sung by his nephew at a party. He immediately requested his young nephew to teach him the song. When asked why he was so eager to learn the song, he supposedly said, "So that having learned it, I may die." True or not, the story illustrates what seems to have been a widespread admiration for Sappho's

The Lyre and the Laurel

According to Margaret Reynolds, in *The Sappho Companion*, Sappho was associated with two specific objects—the lyre and the laurel wreath. According to myth, Apollo, the god of music and poetry, gave the gift of the lyre to his son, Orpheus, who brought it to the human realm. Sappho sang many of her poems accompanied by the lyre and in popular representations of the poet, it became a mirror of her moods. If the strings were broken, Sappho was heart-sick. If they were whole and she able to play, then all was well. Similarly, artists and readers also associated her with the laurel wreath, worn by the winners of ancient games and poetry contests among them. Again, if the wreath was askew on the head of the poet, she was in dire straits, occasionally to the point where the wreath had fallen from her head to be trampled underfoot. Her props became a mode of pathetic fallacy for visual and literary artists.

poetry. It also illustrates what was probably the major means of "publication" of Sappho's songs during her lifetime and in the following century: verbal transmission from one singer to another. There is some indication that by the 5th century B.C., written copies of some of her work may have existed in Athens. Such written copies may have formed the basis for the first edition of her collected works made by scholars at Alexandria during the 3rd century B.C. (see chapter 6).

The Romans also admired Sappho, alluding to her in their own lyric poetry, and in the case of the Roman poets Catullus and Horace in the 1st century B.C., even imitating her poetic meters in Latin and adapting some of her verse to their own use. An obscure Greek poet also of the 1st century B.C., Antipater of Thessaloniki, even composed a poem about the nine "earthly" Muses, in which Sappho is described as "the ornament of the fair-tressed Lesbians" and paid tribute to along with eight other women poets of antiquity.

However, early in the Christian Era, some of the church fathers began to find fault with Sappho, largely because they objected to her celebration of female erotic feelings directed toward females. Tatian, for example, writing in the 2nd century A.D., labels Sappho a "love-crazy female fornicator who even sings about her own licentiousness."

A pagan writer, Lucian, also of the 2nd century A.D., portrays a woman from Lesbos as a scandalous individual who is pretending to be a man. In the section of Lucian's satire (*Dialogi Meretricii* 5) that follows, two prostitutes are conversing with each other; one asks the other (named Leaina) about the details of her affair with the woman from Lesbos:

We hear strange things about you, Leaina—that the rich woman from Lesbos loves you as though she were a man and that you live together and do heaven knows what with each other.... They say that in Lesbos there are masculine-looking women who refuse to have intercourse with men, but who want to be with women as if they themselves were men.

To be sure, this was written as a humorous satire, not a sociological treatise, but it nevertheless contains a long-standing stereotype of lesbians (and, in this case, Lesbians) as fake men.

The elements mentioned by these two critics, one Christian and one pagan, recur in various guises over and over again throughout later discussions of Sappho and Lesbos. There was even a tradition according to which there were *two* Sapphos, one a well-respected poet, the other a prostitute. A medieval dictionary called the *Suda* has one entry that simply identifies Sappho as a poet from Mytilene who leapt off the White Rocks of Leukas out of love for Phaon. A second entry in the same dictionary, however, gives some information about Sappho's family and then adds this censorious remark: "She had three friends and companions, Atthis, Telesippa, and Megara, in connection with whom she had the ill repute of a shameful friendship." The *Suda's* two entries seem to reflect this double tradition of the famous Sappho and the scandalous Sappho.

During later medieval times, Sappho seems to have dropped out of sight, reemerging in the Renaissance as a kind of virginal, aristocratic figure. The English playwright John Lyly, for example, published a play in 1584 called *Sapho and Phao* in which Sappho is presented as a wise, learned, royal figure intended as an allegorical representation of Queen Elizabeth, for whom the play was performed.

Joan DeJean has shown that in the 17th century it was the French translators and biographers who were the most influential in controlling the image of Sappho through editions and translations of her work. Unlike the later, chaste Germanic version of Sappho, the Gallic Sappho of the 17th century was presented as an amorous woman and given a high ranking in the canon of ancient Greek poets. One scholar, Tanneguy Le Fèvre, published an edition of her poetry in 1660, and in 1664 wrote pedagogical notes about her poetry that plainly state (albeit without using any terms such as lesbian) the nature of the female-centered desire expressed in her verse.

During the 18th and 19th centuries, the one complete poem that we have left of Sappho's (the "Hymn to Aphrodite," see chapter 4) was widely translated from Greek into English and various modern European languages. The poem presents a prayer to the goddess of love for assistance in winning the heart of a beloved person. In the original Greek, it is clear that both the narrator (the *I*) of the song and the beloved person are female; nevertheless, this detail was obscured by many translators, who rendered the beloved as *him* instead of *her*, thus transferring the song from a homoerotic context to a heterosexual one.

By the time we get to the Victorian period (the latter two-thirds of the 19th century), under the influence of German classical scholarship Sappho was almost uniformly portrayed as a model of purity. Except for an occasional rebellious Frenchman such as Pierre Lout's, scholars and writers went to great lengths to put her songs into a context (imagined by them) in which the expression of passionate love could be explained in a way that would not be offensive to Victorian moral standards. It was thought, for example, that she was headmistress of a girls' school on Lesbos, and that her songs were chaste send-offs addressed to her pupils as they left the school to be married. Alternatively, another theory, still popular today, was that she was an official religious leader of a cult of female worshipers devoted to Aphrodite.

In the 1950s scholars began to speak cautiously of Sappho's homosexuality, usually taking care to distinguish words from action. In effect, they posited that while Sappho's words suggested lesbian inclinations, whether she was actually a homosexual and whether her words suggested actual "homosexual practices" were questions best left unanswered. Then, of course, scholars influenced by Freudian psychology subjected the fragments of Sappho's poetry to their analysis, usually concluding that her songs revealed various pathological symptoms attributable to the "disease" of homosexuality. (Homosexuality, which had been classified in the United States as an illness in 1952, was not removed from the American Psychiatric Association's list of mental diseases until 1973.)

Today, most people reading what we have left of Sappho's songs are willing to acknowledge the homoerotic context of Sappho's love poems. Whatever theory we may subscribe to as to why Sappho wrote these songs, there is little doubt that she intended to represent female desire for the female, or what we would today call lesbian desire.

three

Women's Roles
in Ancient Greece

Sapho (sic) could fly her impulses like bright
balloons tip-tilting to a morning air
And write about it. Mrs. Browning's heart
Was squeezed in stiff conventions ...
                                    —Amy Lowell, "The Sisters"

IN ORDER TO FILL out our picture of the sort of world in which Sappho may have lived, I turn now to the larger question of the status of ancient Greek women in general. Although we have very limited information indeed about women's lives on the island of Lesbos, we do know something about women's roles elsewhere in Greece, particularly in Athens. We have to be careful not to overgeneralize, however, by assuming that the position of women on Lesbos was necessarily the same in every respect as it was in Athens. Greece in ancient times was not a unified country as it is today, but a collection of independent city-states or *poleis* (plural of *polis*, the root of the English word *political*). These city-states shared a common language that was spoken in a variety of distinctive dialects much more different from each other than, say, American English spoken in Cleveland and British English spoken in London. No doubt these independent city-states did share a similar culture in many respects, but we risk making imperfect and quite possibly incorrect analogies when we try to conjecture what the social practices of a lesser-known city-state might have been on the basis of what we know about a famous place such as Athens.

THE SOURCES OF INFORMATION

With these cautions in mind, what sort of picture emerges when we examine the ancient sources for information about women? As I have already mentioned, most of our sources tend to be androcentric, and we have only a few remains of works by other female writers besides Sappho. Historians writing in ancient times, all of whom were male, conceived of history as a power struggle among the male elite. Hence they generally paid only scant attention to the economic underclasses (male or female), to slaves, or to women. Nevertheless, we are able to glean some information about women's lives from occasional comments made by them and by other male authors, including medical writers.

In addition, two other major kinds of sources are available to us today. Particularly important are the thousands of surviving Athenian vase paintings that portray the daily activities of men and women. The color schemes on these vases are the result of the firing process. In effect, the scene is fired into the clay, so that even if the vase has been broken into pieces, the pieces can be glued back together to reveal the picture that decorated the pot. These durable pots were used for a variety of practical purposes (carrying water, storing olive oil, mixing wine and water, etc.) and were widely exported all over the Mediterranean area, so they survive in large numbers even to the present day.

An additional source of information about women's lives comes in the form of inscriptions, or writing carved into a durable stone like marble. Occasionally a government decree carved into stone will reveal something about the legal status of women, and there are also thousands of surviving tombstone inscriptions that record a woman's name and often some information about her.

By modern American standards, women's lives in Athens would have seemed quite restricted in a number of ways. Generally speaking, even upper-class women had few legal rights and led lives largely confined to their homes, where they were in charge of supervision of home industries like the weaving of material and the manufacturing of clothing. Women were not considered citizens, so they had no opportunity to participate directly in government decisions and were not able to cast votes or serve on juries. Furthermore, formal education in Athens was available only to upper-class boys; girls had to learn whatever skills they needed to acquire on an informal basis at home, taught by their mothers and other female members of the household.

Although Greek epic (Homer's *Iliad* and *Odyssey*) and Greek drama (plays by Aeschylus, Sophocles, Euripides, and Aristophanes) feature a number of strong female characters, it appears that these mythological heroines bore a limited resemblance to the actual women of Athens during the period of the 6th, 5th, and 4th centuries B.C. Aristophanes' comedy *Lysistrata*, in which the women of Athens and Sparta join ranks and organize a sex strike to force their husbands into a peace agreement after the Peloponnesian War had dragged on for two decades, must have based much of its humor in ancient times on role reversal. In other words, in the real world (in which the sexual services of prostitutes would have been readily available, a fact ignored in the play), wives would in fact have had no such power to control the political and military decisions of their husbands. The play is comical because it turns the usual hierarchy of power topsy-turvy and grants the upper hand to women for a change.

A speech by the famous 5th-century B.C. statesman Pericles, preserved and probably embellished by the Greek historian Thucydides (*Peloponnesian War* 2.46), is devoted mostly to praise of the Athenian men who had died in the first year of the Peloponnesian War. At the very end of the speech, after extolling the virtues of the dead and of the city of Athens (described as an "education to all of Greece"), Pericles adds a word of advice to the war widows. He says that "the greatest glory for a woman is to be the least talked about by men, whether as the subject of praise or blame." That statement aptly sums up the marginal status of women in Athens. Rather than participating as equals in the full range of political and social activities open to men, they were to fit into the hierarchy of power in such a way so as to attract as little attention as possible.

WOMEN'S DAILY LIVES IN ATHENS

An upper-class Athenian girl could expect to be married at an early age (15 or so) to a man who would likely be 10 to 15 years her senior. By Athenian marriage custom, a girl had to be provided with a dowry in order for her to marry; girls were thus regarded as a financial burden on the family, and it is thought that female infanticide (accomplished by abandoning the baby outdoors and letting her starve to death) was sometimes practiced in order to reduce the number of female children. Marriages were arranged by the fathers and were probably rarely affairs of the heart.

The young bride was expected to have acquired sufficient household management skills to be able to supervise the home production of clothing by overseeing the spinning, weaving, and sewing activities of slaves and the other female members of the house. She was also in charge of cooking and cleaning. The men and women of the household tended to operate in separate spheres, even to the point of having a separate part of the house reserved as the women's quarters.

The young wife's most important duty, however, was to bear male heirs who could inherit the family property. A woman could not inherit property herself, but could only act as a kind of transmitter of property in the event that she was still unmarried and had no living brothers at the time of her father's death. In that instance, such a woman (known as an *epikleros*, "one attached to the estate") was obliged to marry her nearest male kinsman (e.g., a cousin) so that *he* could inherit the estate by virtue of being the heiress's husband. In this way the property was still kept within the family.

Women's health was often precarious, for the young age at the time of marriage and the emphasis on the need for a male heir meant that young women often began their childbearing years as early as age 15 or 16, before their bodies were fully mature. Childbearing was dangerous business, suffered without benefit of anesthesia or effective ways of dealing with breech deliveries or other complications, and no doubt a high percentage of women died in childbirth or at an early age, exhausted from excessive pregnancies. Women's bodies were generally regarded by medical writers from various parts of the Greek world as inferior versions of male bodies, and medical practice suffered from a number of assumptions based on erroneous theories of female physiology. The female role in reproduction was not adequately understood, for many of the ancient Greek medical writers thought that the womb was merely a kind of safe receptacle in which the male seed could be planted and then grow into the child to be born. (Aristotle thought that women were unable to produce semen because they were by nature "cold" compared to males.) They also thought that a woman was most likely to become pregnant through intercourse just after her menstrual period had ended, whereas today we know that in fact the most fertile period occurs during days 14 to 16 of the 28-day cycle. In addition, they believed that women tended to suffer various emotional and physical problems as the result of a "wandering womb," and they devised all sorts of strange remedies to see to it that the womb (*hystera* in Greek) returned to its proper location. It is to this "wandering womb" theory that we owe the English word *hysteria*.

Despite all this emphasis on childbearing and on household management, there is some evidence that at least in 4th-century Athens, women were occasionally employed outside the home. One tombstone inscription memorializes a midwife-physician named Phanostrate, and another honors a nurse (that is, a woman who nursed and cared for the children of a wealthy family) named Melitta. Manumission inscriptions record the professions of former slaves who had become freedwomen, the majority of whom seem to have been in the wool-working trade.

For the majority of upper-class women, however, perhaps the greatest opportunity for freedom from the confines of the house came in the form of participation in the religious festivals of the community. Particularly important were festivals connected with the fertility of the earth, which was closely associated with female fertility in general. At Athens there was an annual autumn festival in honor of Demeter (also known to us by her Roman name, Ceres), the goddess of grain and the mother of Persephone. This festival, which was restricted to female participants, was called the Thesmophoria and went on for three days at the time of the autumn sowing of seeds to ensure their proper growth. Only free women could participate in the rituals, and they were obliged to abstain from sex just before and during the festival. Since the Thesmophoria was restricted to women, the male authors who speak of it are either not very well informed as to what went on, or are reticent out of religious scruples. From what little we know, however, evidently the rituals involved digging up various objects that had been buried in the ground during an earlier, summer festival, including the remains of sacrificial piglets, models of snakes (symbols of the earth's fertility), and representations of male sexual organs. These sacred objects were then scattered in the fields along with the seeds to promote the fertility of the crops.

Most of the religious festivals in the area of Athens were open to both male and female participants. One of the most important of these was the Panathenaea, celebrated annually (and every fourth year on a grand scale) in honor of the patron goddess of the city, Athena (in Roman mythology, Minerva). Young girls took part in various aspects of the festival, including carrying sacred baskets in a procession, and for the Greater Panathenaea (the one held every fourth year), girls and women

wove a new robe that was presented to a sacred wooden statue
of Athena housed in a building near the Parthenon, her temple
on top of the acropolis. From our sources we know that the
Panathenaic festival, which lasted several days, included as well
various athletic and musical contests, but these were open only
to male participants.

Another important religious festival in the area was held at
nearby Eleusis in honor of Demeter and her daughter Persephone. The Eleusinian mysteries, as they were called, celebrated
the death and rebirth of the grain, and also promised a similar
eventual rebirth for all people (including men and women, free
or slave) who took part in the mysteries. According to Greek
myth, the young Persephone was stolen away by force one day
while she was picking flowers, to be the bride of Hades, the god
of the Underworld. Demeter went into mourning for her
absent daughter, with the result that the crops died and nothing
would bloom. Eventually, a compromise was agreed upon, and
Persephone spent two-thirds of the year with her mother,
during which time the crops flourished, and only one-third
with Hades, when the crops died.

Because the details of the Eleusinian mysteries were known
only to the participants, who were sworn to secrecy, our knowledge of these rituals is insufficient. But we do know that
women served in a variety of roles as different types of priest-
esses at Eleusis. In fact, the events at Eleusis were recorded
under the name and year of service of whoever was the chief
priestess of Demeter at the time.

It is clear that in Athens, at any rate, the various religious festivals offered the women of the city the chance to mingle with
people other than the members of their immediate household,
so that the typical Athenian wife did not live in total "oriental
seclusion," as such a restricted existence is sometimes called.
However, Athenian wives certainly did not have the kind of

freedom available to the most well-to-do members of a class of women called *hetairai* (companions). Prostitution was legal in Athens, and slave women (and boys) worked at government-owned brothels to service the male clientele. Freedwomen and foreign-born women, many of whom were highly educated, could work under their own auspices as intellectual and sexual companions for the wealthy men who could afford to pay the price. The most famous of these higher-class *hetairai* was Aspasia of Miletus, the companion of the statesman Pericles. Although prostitution was legal, it was certainly not regarded as respectable, and no freeborn Athenian woman would have even thought of entering such a profession.

Such, in bare outline, is the information we have about women's lives in Athens. Curiously, although our sources (particularly Plato) reveal a great deal about what we would label homosexual behavior among males, we hear literally nothing about similar relationships among females. Athenian vase paintings portray sexual encounters between a teenage boy and an adult male in large numbers; many such vases (often inscribed with the word kalos [handsome], and the name of the younger partner) were given as courtship gifts by the older man to the younger. Other vase paintings reflect some of the many stories in Greek mythology that represent erotic relationships between a male deity or hero and an ordinary mortal youth. Among the most famous of these are Zeus's love for the youth Ganymede, Apollo's love for Hyacinthus (a handsome young man from Sparta whom the god accidentally killed with a discus), and Hercules' love for the boy Hylas. But neither literature nor art produced at Athens ever alludes to what we would call female homosexuality. It must have occurred, especially given the gender segregation of daily life, but was probably regarded as so slight a threat to the existing hierarchical system and to the childbearing role of women that it was simply ignored altogether.

WOMEN'S LIVES ON LESBOS

When we turn from Athens to Lesbos to see how some of this picture of women's lives might apply there, we are on much shakier ground because of the paucity of evidence from the island. However, we are probably safe in assuming a few generalizations. For example, there is little doubt that women were treated as noncitizens on Lesbos, for nowhere in ancient Greece do we hear of women having the same rights as men. The division of labor between males and females was probably also similar, so that girls were no doubt trained in the same kinds of home industries (particularly spinning and weaving) as they were in Athens and in other Greek city-states. Upper-class girls were probably expected to learn how to supervise such household activities.

Unfortunately we have no way of knowing with any certainty how unusual it might have been on Lesbos for a woman to write poetry. However, there is nothing among the surviving fragments of Sappho's songs to indicate that she thought of herself as some sort of isolated phenomenon, and, indeed, she

Visions of Sappho

Sappho has appeared on hundreds of works of arts, from pottery to book covers, portraits to an infamous issue of Playboy magazine. Again, in keeping with her changing status within public Puritanism, she alternates between being a lady of higher learning, clothed with books surrounding her, to bare-breasted or nude, a representative of lesbian love. Interestingly, in the majority of representations up until the 18th century, the poet tended to be given the garments of the contemporary time. With her clothes, her appearance changed as well, sometimes tall and slim, other times short and heavy. For a small sample of art, see *www.beloit.edu/~classics/museum205/Sappho_art_museum205.htm*.

seems to mention other women whom she considers inspired—in varying degrees—by the Muses (see chapter 6). Although we know that some ancient male poets (like the 5th-century Pindar, who wrote odes in celebration of victorious athletes) received commissions for their songs, we have no information at all about the economic aspects, if any, of Sappho's role as a poet.

It is also clear from remarks in the poetry of both Sappho and Alcaeus (even if we do not interpret them on a strictly literal level) that religious ceremonies played an important part in people's daily lives. Besides frequent mention of Aphrodite, the goddess of love, we find references to Hera (in Roman mythology, Juno), the Graces, Hermes (Mercury in Roman mythology), Zeus (Jupiter), Leto, the twins Castor and Pollux (Gemini), and Dionysus (Bacchus). It seems reasonable to assume that girls and women, as in Athens, had ample opportunity to take part in various religious festivals on the island in honor of these and other deities. In one of the fragments of Alcaeus's songs (frag. 130b V.), he speaks of living in some remote part of the island during a time of political upheaval and of being near a sacred precinct "where Lesbian women walk about trailing their gowns and being judged for their beauty, while the wondrous sound of the women's sacred cry every year echoes all around." Alcaeus's description seems to imply that he had witnessed some kind of annual religious festival in which the women of Lesbos played a prominent role. Evidently the ceremonies included a beauty contest, as well as ritual cries uttered by the assembled group of women.

From the fragments of Alcaeus's songs we can reconstruct a fairly clear picture of aristocratic male clubs formed for social, political, and religious purposes. Such a male association was called a *hetaireia* (an organization of companions). Since Sappho describes her friends as *hetairai* (companions)—here the word evidently does not refer to prostitutes as in Athens—

some scholars today conjecture that perhaps Sappho sang her songs for a similar group of female associates. We have no way of knowing for sure who might have been in such a group, but there is some indication (in sources from many centuries after Sappho's lifetime, to be sure) that many of the women whom Sappho calls by name in her songs came to Lesbos from cities on or near the coast of the nearby mainland of Asia Minor, cities such as Miletus and Colophon. In one of the fragments (frag. 96 V.), she speaks of a woman formerly connected with her immediate circle on Lesbos as having gone away to Sardis, the main city of Lydia. It appears, then, that for whatever reason, there was a fair amount of coming and going in Sappho's circle, and that its members moved freely between island and mainland.

Whether this hypothetical circle to which Sappho and these friends belonged was in fact a kind of school or other more formal association such as a religious cult, we can only guess. Was Sappho the head of whatever the association might have been, whether as teacher or priestess? I myself would hesitate to say, since there is so little solid evidence to go on. In any case, it may well be that the women of Lesbos and of neighboring cities had greater freedom of movement and of association than their counterparts in Athens. In the chapters that follow, I will leave aside the difficult question of the exact context of Sappho's songs, and try to focus instead on the songs themselves for what they can tell us about the representation of lesbian desire.

four

Sappho and the Goddess of Love

Come to me now also, release me from
harsh cares; accomplish as many things as my heart desires
to accomplish; and you yourself
be my fellow soldier.

—Sappho Fr. 1. V.

HOW IS IT THAT WE HAVE anything left at all of what Sappho wrote? A Byzantine scholar named Tzetzes, writing in the 12th century A.D., alludes to the fact that even in his day, time had destroyed the works of Sappho. There are also reports of deliberate destruction of her poetry; according to one legend, Pope Gregory VII (11th century A.D.) was supposed to have ordered her poems to be cast into the flames. Unlike the works of more recent writers, for which we often have first and second drafts in the authors' own handwriting, together with different versions of printed editions of their published material, in the case of Sappho and other ancient authors we must depend on much less reliable and much less complete sources.

As far as Sappho's poetry is concerned today, we have three types of sources in which it has been preserved: (1) manuscripts of later authors who quote her poetry from memory or from editions available to them at the time, (2) fragments of papyrus copies of her poems found in Egypt, and (3) in one case at least, a bit of one of her poems scratched onto a piece of broken pottery (an ostracon, or potsherd, the scrap paper of the ancient world).

If you wanted to see what Sappho's poems look like in the original Greek, you would not have to decipher these sources yourself. You would simply go to a large library and find a modern edition of her poetry. To prepare such a volume, the editor sifts through the original sources (or photocopies of them) and studies the work of other scholars who have interpreted the evidence; then, in the case of conflicting evidence, the editor makes an educated guess as to what Sappho probably wrote. Usually a modern edition is formatted in such a way that the reconstructed Greek text is printed at the top of the page in large type, with explanatory matter and alternate versions of problematic words in smaller type at the bottom of the page.

The first category of sources, the manuscripts of authors who lived and wrote well after Sappho's time but who quote her poems, is the source of the one complete song of Sappho's left to us, the "Hymn to Aphrodite". By manuscripts, I do not mean these ancient authors' own handwriting, but rather copies of copies passed down over the centuries. These were done on parchment, a writing surface made from animal skins that is very durable. We owe much to Arab scholars in Spain and to medieval monks in Europe who laboriously recopied earlier works by hand. (Remember that the printing press did not exist until Johannes Gutenberg invented movable type in about 1440.) The existing copies of these ancient authors' works, then, preserve occasional pieces of Sappho's poetry whenever the author chooses to quote her work in order to comment on it or prove a point. Unfortunately, many such quotations are extremely short, for the author might only have been interested in a peculiar word of Sappho's or a quaint expression that she used.

The second category, the papyrus fragments from Egypt, is the source of many of the more recent discoveries of Sappho's songs, within about the last hundred years. Papyrus, made from the fibers of the Egyptian papyrus plant, was a durable writing surface in ancient times. (The word *papyrus* is the origin of our English word paper.) Pieces of ancient literature copied onto papyrus have turned up in Egypt in mummy wrappings and in junk piles dating from the Hellenistic period—for example, in scraps thrown down a dried-up, abandoned well. These papyrus finds from Egypt, even in their tattered state, have been extremely helpful in expanding our collection of Sappho's songs. In one or two cases we even have a dog-eared, weather-beaten papyrus version of a poem that can be used to help fill out a partial manuscript quotation of the same poem.

The third category, the potsherd, is really only a fluke, for we have but one fragment of Sappho's poetry preserved in this manner. This is another song addressed to Aphrodite, fragment 2 discussed below. The potsherd version of the song, despite its many spelling errors, allowed scholars to fill out a rather approximate partial quotation by an ancient writer.

Needless to say, all three types of sources are tricky to decipher, for the copies are fraught with smudges, gaps, rips, copyists' errors, and other defects that make them hard to read. Trained specialists are required to do the job: paleographers to interpret the parchment manuscripts, papyrologists to decipher the bits of papyrus, and epigraphists to decode writing inscribed onto surfaces such as stone or broken pottery scraps. The durability of ancient and medieval writing surfaces does make one wonder what will be preserved a couple of thousand years from now. Paper, microfilm, and computer disks all seem rather flimsy by comparison!

Lesbianism as Mental Illness

According to Bernadette Brooten in her book, *Love Between Women*, medical writer, Soranos of Ephesos (2nd c. A.D.) argued that women who actively pursued other women were mentally ill, and their pursual of women a masculine pursuit. As such, the women seduced by other women were not to be faulted; they were maintaining their traditional positions as passive partners in a sexual encounter. The "masculine" women, the tribades, when in remission from their mental illness were believed to accuse other women of being tribades. He suggested "mind control" as a form of treatment that might eventually cure the "disease" entirely (Brooten 143–55).

THE "HYMN TO APHRODITE"

The one completely preserved song of Sappho's left to us today is a beautiful prayer addressed to Aphrodite, the goddess of love. We have it today because an ancient literary critic admired it so much that he quoted the entire poem. Like a modern song, it was written in stanza form, and presumably each stanza was sung (with the accompaniment of a lyre) to the same tune. Unfortunately, we have no ancient Greek music from earlier than the 4th century B.C., so we have only a vague idea of the musical aspects of Sappho's poetry. We do know that later Greek writers and vase painters associated both Sappho and her compatriot Alcaeus with a long-armed type of seven-stringed lyre called the *barbitos*. We can safely assume that both poets performed their own songs and accompanied themselves on this type of lyre.

In reading this poem, it will help you to know that Sappho is toying slightly with the standard pattern of an ancient Greek prayer. If you were an ancient Greek person praying to a deity, you would (1) address the god or goddess by name, (2) give a few identifying labels (to make sure you were getting in touch with the right deity), (3) remind the deity briefly of your previous relationship with her or him, and then (4) devote the bulk of your prayer to stating your present request for help. As you read the following translation of the song, which is a request to Aphrodite for help on the "battlefield" of love, see if you can tell how Sappho plays with the expected proportions devoted to each of these four sections of a prayer. I suggest that you read the translation slowly and out loud, so as to approximate an ancient performance of the song:

Fragment 1 V.

O immortal Aphrodite of the many-colored throne,
child of Zeus, weaver of wiles, I beseech you,

do not overwhelm me in my heart
with anguish and pain, O Mistress,

But come hither, if ever at another time
hearing my cries from afar
you heeded them, and leaving the home of your father
came, yoking your golden

Chariot: beautiful, swift sparrows
drew you above the black earth
whirling their wings thick and fast,
from heaven's ether through mid-air.

Suddenly they had arrived; but you, O Blessed Lady,
with a smile on your immortal face,
asked what I had suffered again and
why I was calling again

And what I was most wanting to happen for me
in my frenzied heart: "Whom again shall I persuade
to come back into friendship with you? Who,
O Sappho, does you injustice?

"For if indeed she flees, soon will she pursue,
and though she receives not your gifts, she will give them,
and if she loves not now, soon she will love,
even against her will."

Come to me now also, release me from
harsh cares; accomplish as many things as my heart desires
to accomplish; and you yourself
be my fellow soldier.

As you have noticed, this "Hymn to Aphrodite" (as we generally call it now) contains all four of the expected sections. However, instead of just getting through the preliminaries and spending most of the prayer on what the petitioner wants assistance with now (winning over a reluctant potential lover, it would seem), Sappho devotes the whole middle part of the song (from "if ever" at the beginning of stanza 2 to "against her will" at the end of the next-to-last stanza) to the previous relationship between herself and the goddess. The vignette describing the past instance of Aphrodite's speeding down from Mount Olympus to Sappho's rescue is so vividly portrayed that we almost forget that it is not occurring at the present moment. In fact, however, the middle five stanzas of this seven-stanza song deal with Sappho's exchanges with the goddess of love *in the past*. Only in the very last stanza does Sappho get back to her actual request: "Come to me now also ..."

Part of the song's charm involves the detail with which Sappho describes Aphrodite's past journey to assist her: the golden chariot, the whirring wings of the sparrows which drew it (sparrows were closely associated by the Greeks with fertility, hence their connection with Aphrodite as goddess of love), and the goddess's series of concerned questions for Sappho upon her arrival.

It was this part of the song—the series of questions—that presented a problem for some of the 18th- and 19th-century translators (see chapter 2). In the original Greek it is perfectly clear that Aphrodite is asking Sappho (addressed by name in stanza 5) "What *woman* is causing you problems this time?" Even though we need not take the poem as a literal description of what actually happened to Sappho last Tuesday night, so to speak, the song does clearly speak of a homoerotic situation; the narrator of the song, "Sappho," according to her report of a past conversation with Aphrodite, was in love with a woman who was not in love with her. But some of the translators of the song before the 20th century disguised the gender of the beloved person so that the beginning of the next-to-last stanza, for example, came out as "For if indeed *he* flees, soon *he* will pursue," and so on. In effect, they censored the song, removing it from its homoerotic context and fitting it instead into a heterosexual one.

Although the wording is subtle by modern standards, there is no doubt that the song is talking about unrequited erotic love, not just a falling-out between female friends (another line of approach for nervous readers who have wanted to "deleslbianize" the song). In the first place, one does not call upon the goddess of love for help in mere matters of compromise and diplomacy, but for matters of the human heart. Secondly, the Greek word for friendship in stanza 5 is much more inclusive than the English word, encompassing as it does both familial love (e.g., between mother and child) and erotic love (between husband and wife, between a man and another man, or between a woman and another woman). Finally, the reference to giving gifts in the next-to-last stanza is a clear allusion to the Greek custom of the exchange of love tokens, as, for example, the special vases given by a man to his younger male lover (see chapter 3). Given the fact that in ancient Greece marriages were arranged, and were primarily focused on economic considerations like the preservation of family property, it is perhaps not surprising that such gift giving and other aspects of courtship and romance were more often reserved for homosexual unions and liaisons.

Another charming aspect of Sappho's "Hymn to Aphrodite" is its emphasis on the close relationship between goddess and petitioner. Aphrodite is hardly a frightening deity here. She arrives with a smile (of indulgence?) on her face, and says, in effect, "Well, dear, what is it *this* time?" It would seem that

"Sappho" (again, remember that poets can make themselves into their own fictional or quasi-fictional characters) has had heart-to-heart talks with Aphrodite on any number of occasions in the past. The repetition of the contact between goddess and mortal serves to underscore their close relationship. The goddess seems to be a kind of antidote to the painful aspects of love, what Sappho refers to elsewhere as bittersweetness; the "Sappho" narrator relies on Aphrodite's power both to soothe the heart and to bring about the heart's desire.

Curiously, Sappho chooses to end this song with a military image. When she asks Aphrodite in the last line of the poem to be her "fellow soldier," she suddenly introduces the idea of battle into the song. Such a notion seems especially strange when we recall that in the earliest Greek literature that we have, Homer's *Iliad* (5.330–430), Aphrodite is without doubt a wimp. Stripped of her powers as a pre-Greek earth mother goddess who no doubt originally resembled other Near Eastern fertility goddesses like Cybele and Ishtar, the Homeric Aphrodite has clearly been diminished by Greek patriarchal religious structures. She gets wounded in the fighting and limps home in tears to her mother and Zeus, her father. She doesn't even have her own chariot for the trip to Mount Olympus—she has to borrow her brother's vehicle. Based on her characterization in the *Iliad*, she is not the goddess you would pick to be your comrade in arms. It may be that what Sappho is doing in this song is deliberately rejecting the old Homeric values, the blood-and-guts heroism of hand-to-hand combat between warriors. In effect she is here announcing a different kind of battle and a different Aphrodite—one that perhaps reflects aspects of the goddess's original status as a powerful earth mother deity. In a between-the-lines message Sappho may even be proclaiming that just as Homer was the champion of the old heroic code, so she, Sappho, is the champion of the new. Follow me, she is saying—make love, not war!

It is from this one remaining complete song of Sappho's that we must imagine what the fragments of everything else we have left would have been like had they survived intact. For a song that would only have taken perhaps five or six minutes to perform, it has everything: majesty of expression (in the opening address to the goddess), beauty of description (the goddess's descent to earth), balance and tension (the serenity of the immortal goddess contrasting with the suffering of the mortal narrator), and dramatic dialogue (the implied conversation in the past between the goddess, whose words are quoted, and "Sappho," whose replies are left to the hearer's imagination). To have heard the song performed with musical accompaniment 2,600 years ago—perhaps outdoors in a shady precinct sacred to Aphrodite on a hill overlooking the Aegean Sea—would have been a truly splendid experience.

AN INVITATION TO APHRODITE

We have another lovely poem addressed to Aphrodite (who was also called the Cyprian, referring to her birthplace, the island of Cyprus) that appears to be almost complete. At any rate, enough of it remains for us to get some idea of its beautiful description of a sacred precinct. This is the poem that was scratched (perhaps by a schoolboy) onto a potsherd that has been dated to the 3rd century B.C. Although some of the poem had been known before the potsherd was discovered, it was not until 1937 that the publication of the potsherd enabled us to have this more complete version:

Fragment 2 V.

Hither to me from Crete, to this holy

temple, where your lovely grove
of apple trees is, and the altars
smoke with frankincense.

Herein cold water rushes through
apple boughs, and the whole place is shaded
with roses, and sleep comes down
from rustling leaves.

Herein a meadow where horses graze
blooms with spring flowers, and the winds
blow gently ...

Here, O Cyprian, taking [garlands],
in golden cups gently pour forth
nectar mingled together with our
festivities ...

This lovely song, at least in the portion remaining, seems to focus on sacred space. The narrator invites Aphrodite to leave the island of Crete and come to her temple on Lesbos. It is a request for an epiphany, that is, for the deity to make her presence seen and felt by her worshipers, who seem (in the last stanza) to be taking part in some kind of sacred ritual.

The emphasis in the fragment is on the holiness of the area around the temple, which Sappho describes with delicious images. Notice how she appeals to at least four of our five senses at once—sight (the grove of apples trees, the temple, the altars, the meadow and its flowers), smell (the frankincense filling the air with its fragrance), touch (the cold water and cooling shade), and sound (the rushing stream, the tree leaves rustling in the wind). Even taste is implied as the fragment breaks off, for the goddess is invited to pour nectar into golden cups to drink. According to Homer's *Iliad* and *Odyssey*, ambrosia and nectar are the special food and drink of the gods.

This is the song that had led some scholars to suppose that perhaps Sappho was an official priestess of Aphrodite, and that she is calling upon the goddess to attend the religious ceremonies that she, in her official capacity, has organized in the goddess's honor. Such an interpretation is certainly possible, but unfortunately we have no way of knowing exactly what the occasion of the song might have been. It could have been written to be sung for a group of Sappho's friends to remind them of a place sacred to Aphrodite; or it might have been sung by Sappho as a participant at a festival in honor of the goddess; or it might be pure fiction—drawn from the religious experience of archaic Lesbos, to be sure, but fiction nevertheless.

Perhaps the most compelling feature of the apple grove song is its mesmerizing effect on the hearer, which I have tried to capture in the sound of my translation. Besides the repeated elements of the sentences ("Hither ... Herein ... Herein ... Here"), the original Greek text is filled with *s* sounds, which seem to imitate the rustling leaves. How wonderful to imagine that in this sacred space—safe and sound from outside intrusion—sleep descends from trees as if by magic.

Aphrodite is mentioned in several other very short fragments of Sappho's poems, and it is clear that if we had a more intact collection of poetry, the goddess of love would figure prominently among Sappho's cast of characters. Whether or not Sappho was ever actually a priestess in the service of Aphrodite, she clearly was Aphrodite's servant in the sense that she honored her in song.

five

Sappho's Lesbian Love Songs

The isles of Greece, the isles of Greece!
Where burning Sappho loved and sung.
                    —Lord Byron, "Don Juan"

THIS CHAPTER TURNS to the four most famous love songs among the remaining fragments of Sappho's work. It is important to remember that, unlike the "Hymn to Aphrodite" examined in the previous chapter, all four of these songs are fragmentary. We have to be conscious of the fact that any overarching conclusions we may draw might conceivably be proven wrong were we lucky enough to find a new papyrus that could be used to fill out a missing portion. Such a discovery is not completely beyond the realm of possibility. One ancient writer of comedies named Menander, famous in his day at the end of the 4th century B.C., was known in modern times only through fragments and Roman imitations of his work until the mid-20th century, when publication of papyrus discoveries brought to light one entire play and substantial portions of five others. We can always hope that similar discoveries will expand our meager collection of Sappho's songs.

SAPPHO'S BROKEN TONGUE: FRAGMENT 31 V.

The following song of Sappho's, which is unfortunately missing its final stanza or two, is probably her most famous piece next to the "Hymn to Aphrodite" (see chapter 4). Like the "Hymn to Aphrodite," this song was preserved for us by an ancient literary critic who admired it. The song's fame is due partly to the fact that the Roman poet Catullus made an adaptation of it into Latin in the 1st century B.C., and his version became one of the better known pieces of Latin lyric poetry.

As the song opens, the unidentified narrator (whom we shall call "Sappho," but remember that the poem is not necessarily autobiographical) is describing a man and a woman sitting close to each other and talking. The man soon disappears, and the remainder of the song focuses on the narrator's intensely passionate reaction every time she sees this particular woman. The "Sappho" narrator is so affected by the sight of this woman that she suffers everything from total speechlessness (a bad problem for a poet-singer!) to a near-death experience:

Fragment 31 V.

He seems to me to be like the gods
—whatever man sits opposite you
and close by hears you
talking sweetly

And laughing charmingly, which
makes the heart within my breast take flight;
for the instant I look upon you, I cannot anymore
speak one word,

But in silence my tongue is broken, a fine
fire at once runs under my skin,
with my eyes I see not one thing, my ears
buzz,

Cold sweat covers me, trembling
seizes my whole body, I am more moist than grass;
I seem to be little short
of dying ...

But all must be ventured ...

Believe it or not, this poem, burning with the intensity of one woman's erotic desire for another, was explained at the turn of the century as a wedding song! The man and the woman of the opening stanza were taken to be the groom and bride, and the rest of the song was interpreted as a chaste farewell expression of love as Sappho bids good-bye to her pupil, who is leaving

Sappho's school upon her marriage. Such an interpretation of course removes the song from a lesbian context and puts it instead safely into a heterosexual framework. It desexualizes and delesbianizes the song and puts it into a context that was acceptable to readers who thought that Sappho was a great Greek poet, and that as such, she would not have even thought of expressing "inappropriate" ideas. Never mind that "appropriate" and "inappropriate" were defined according to the patriarchal, heterosexual standards of Victorian-era morality.

Another heterosexualized slant has been given to the song in more recent interpretations that put considerable emphasis on the man of the opening stanza and interpret the poem as a statement of Sappho's jealousy of him for being close to the woman. According to this reading, whenever Sappho sees the *two of them* talking (this despite the fact that the Greek for you in line 7 is singular, not plural), she is stricken with symptoms of jealousy. One Freudian interpretation even went so far as to say that the "symptoms" listed in the poem corresponded closely to modern clinical observations of a homosexual anxiety attack. According to this jealousy interpretation, the man of the opening stanza is still dominant throughout the song, for he is in effect the cause of Sappho's symptoms. For this reading, the symptoms are usually thought to include being "greener than grass" (stanza 4), a slight misinterpretation of what the original Greek says, namely, "more moist than grass." Such a misreading fits conveniently into the jealousy theory, since today we tend to associate the color green with envy.

It is quite possible, however (and indeed preferable, I think), to read this song in a strictly homoerotic context. In a homoerotic interpretation, the man of the opening stanza merely provides a point of contrast to the narrator, and once he has served that purpose, he drops out of view. Whereas the man ("whatever man sits opposite you") is calmly godlike in response to the woman, the "Sappho" narrator is completely overwhelmed every time she sees her.

The language describing the narrator's reaction is very strong indeed: her heart flutters (a symptom associated with erotic desire elsewhere in Sappho's poetry), and she is stricken with speechlessness. In fact she is not just speechless—her very organ of speech (the tongue) is itself broken. She feels a fire under her skin, her eyes are blind, and her ears hear nothing but a buzzing sound like the noise of a whirligig that you spin around your head on a string. The sensations continue to mount in intensity: she is covered all over with sweat, her whole body trembles, and she is more moist than tender young shoots of grass (the

Radclyffe Hall

In 1928, Radclyffe Hall's *The Well of Loneliness* was brought on trial for obscenity due to its depiction of lesbian love. Many of the modernist intellectuals defended the book, E.M. Forster and Virginia Woolf most publicly. The two wrote a public protest letter and submitted it to *Nation & Athenaeum*, where it appeared on September 8, 1928, after the publisher, Jonathan Cape, had been asked by the Home Secretary to withdraw the book. The case went to court, where Virginia Woolf, George Bernard Shaw, Mary MacCarthy, Hugh Walpole, and E.M. Forster were prepared to testify on behalf of the work's literary merits and the necessity of freedom of the press (Leaska 279–280). When the case came before the Chief Magistrate, he alone ruled it obscene and lacking in literary merit, using phrases like "unnatural tendencies" and "horrible practices" (Reynolds 338). A week later, the book was seized and destroyed upon the order of the court. An appeal made in December of 1928 was dismissed (Leaska 279–280). Woolf, never a fan of the book, wrote, "Our thoughts centre upon Sapphism, we have to uphold the morality of that *Well* of all that's stagnant and luke warm and neither one thing or the other."

poet is not explicit here, but her words suggest the vaginal moisture of desire). Finally, her reaction is of such intensity that she feels as though she is dying—a common poetic metaphor in later literature for orgasm. Then, alas, the song breaks off with some kind of generalization that perhaps formed the final stanza.

Despite the lack of specific reference to sexual organs (which the Greeks generally referred to in literature only in comedy), this poem is an exquisite description of the bodily effects of lesbian sexual desire. It is no wonder that the Victorian interpreters of the song were so concerned to co-opt it back into the framework of marriage, for in its unadulterated state it constitutes a serious challenge to heterosexual dominance.

THE MOST BEAUTIFUL THING ON EARTH: FRAGMENT 16 V.

Another love song of Sappho's survives in what is probably almost complete form, except for some missing words in the next-to-last stanza. The origin of this song is a papyrus, and the edges of the papyrus are so dog-eared at this point that we cannot be certain what words began and ended the lines. Imagine taking a two-and-a-half-inch newspaper column and ripping off a half-inch or so from both sides, and you will have some idea of the problems that papyrologists face in trying to reconstruct precious finds like this one.

In this song, Sappho is following a formula frequently found elsewhere in Greek literature in which the author gives a list of things, saving the best for last. Often, as here, the list is of a series of opinions, and what the author thinks is the best opinion is reserved for the final place in the list. In this case, the opinions answer the question "What is the most beautiful thing on earth?" The answer, in Sappho's view, is "what one loves." She proves her point with two examples, one from myth (the story of Helen of Troy) and one from her own experience (her love for a woman called Anaktoria in the song):

Fragment 16 V.

Some say that the most beautiful thing
upon the black earth is an army of horsemen;
others, of infantry; still others, of ships;
but I say it is what one loves.

It is completely easy to make this
intelligible to everyone; for the woman
who far surpassed all mortals in beauty,
Helen, left her most brave husband

And sailed off to Troy, nor did she
remember at all her child
or her dear parents; but [the Cyprian]
led her away....

[All of which] has now reminded me
of Anaktoria, who is not here.

Her lovely walk and the bright sparkle of her face
I would rather look upon than
all the Lydian chariots
and full-armed infantry.
[*This may be the end of the poem*]

One reason for the assumption that the song is likely to have ended at the close of stanza 5 is the sense of completion we feel upon finding the comparison between Anaktoria and the army of Lydia. After all, the song begins with military references—

the cavalry, infantry, and naval forces mentioned in stanza 1. Many scholars today think that the circular pattern illustrated by stanza 1 and stanza 5 (a poetic technique known as ring composition) is a likely sign of completeness.

The military imagery with which the song opens (and evidently closes) is interesting for several reasons. First of all, it sets the stage for the mythological example that Sappho uses to prove her point about what the most beautiful thing in the world is. The story of Helen is after all the story of the Trojan War, during which the Greeks fought the Trojans for ten long years to win back Helen.

Helen was the beautiful wife of the Greek king Menelaus. In Homer's version, she was abducted by the Trojan prince Paris and taken off to live with him at Troy. Hers was the face that launched a thousand ships, for in retaliation the Greeks organized a massive naval expedition and set sail across the Aegean Sea to the northern coast of Asia Minor (now Turkey), not far, in fact, from the island of Lesbos. There they mounted a full-scale attack against the city of Troy in order to win Helen back.

In Sappho's version in fragment 16, the emphasis is not (as in Homer) on the response of the Greek men to the presumed abduction, but rather on Helen's desire for the unnamed Paris. Sappho describes Helen's departure not as forced but as voluntary (with a little help from the Cyprian, that is, Aphrodite), based on a desire so strong that she willingly abandoned not only Menelaus but also her parents and her child by Menelaus. The whole focus of this portion of the song is on the active desire of Helen for what she loves, that is, the Trojan Paris. Many modern readers have found the example puzzling or jarring, but that is because they are somehow expecting Helen to be (as indeed she usually is in Homer and elsewhere) a beautiful *object*. In Sappho's account, she is a *subject*, not an object. She happens to be beautiful, to be sure, but she is an active subject in pursuit of what *she* desires, what *she* regards as the most beautiful thing on earth.

The military references at the opening of the song are also interesting because they represent a point of view that the author rejects. In fact Sappho rejects the notion of military splendor twice—or at least she twice rejects the notion that an army or a naval fleet could constitute the most beautiful thing on earth. The first rejection occurs at the end of stanza 1, where she asserts her own view: "but I say it is what one loves."

The second rejection comes at the apparent end of the song, where the narrator proclaims that she would rather behold the absent Anaktoria than all the military paraphernalia in the world (or, more precisely, in neighboring Lydia on the coast of Asia Minor). I think it can be argued that Sappho is again indirectly asserting her status as a kind of superior Homer, as she did in the "Hymn to Aphrodite." The old Homer may have thought that it was worth spending hundreds and hundreds of hexameter verses on military troops, equipment, tactics, and carnage, but the new Sappho-Homer knows better. She will sing of love, not war.

THE WOMAN WHO HAS GONE AWAY TO LYDIA: FRAGMENT 96 V.

The importance of the mainland to the island of Lesbos is hinted at as well in the fragments of the next love song we will examine. Fragment 96 is preserved for us, along with several other bits of Sappho's poetry, in a parchment dated to the 6th century A.D. The song, composed in three-line stanzas, is apparently addressed to a woman named Atthis, and seems to be a kind of consolation poem for her, offering solace over the absence of an unnamed woman who has gone away to the country of Lydia on the mainland. The bulk of the fragment consists of a beautiful simile involving a comparison between

the departed woman and the moon. At the opening of the fragment, there seems to be mention of Sardis, the chief city of
Lydia. Evidently the woman who has gone away to Lydia is pic-
tured as thinking about Lesbos and how much she used to
enjoy Atthis's singing:

Fragment 96 V.

... [Sardis?]
Often turning her mind here ...

[She honored you]
like an easily recognized goddess,
she rejoiced especially in your song.

But now she stands out among the Lydian women
as after sunset
the rosy-fingered moon

Surpasses all the stars; the light
spreads over the salty sea
equally as over the many-flowered fields.

And the dew grows beautifully liquid
and roses and tender chervil
flourish, and flowery honey-lotus

But she, roaming about far and wide,
remembers gentle Atthis with desire;
her gentle heart is surely heavy [because of your fate].

... to come ...

I will return to the simile about the moon in a moment, but first I want to look at the theme of absence and desire suggested by the song's framework. One can examine the theme on two levels—one more literal, the other more metaphoric. On the literal level, the poem seems to imply the mobility of the women in Sappho's circle and the relative ease of exchange between island and mainland (see chapters 1, 2, and 3). Given such mobility, it would not be surprising to find love songs on the subject of "She's Gone Away and Left Me."

On a more metaphoric level, however, this particular song can be read as a statement about the interrelationship between absence, desire, and memory. Longing is most acutely felt when the person longed for is not present (see the discussion of fragment 16, page 76). But in order to feel such longing one must rely on memory—the memory of what it was like to be in the absent person's presence. Despite the pain of separation, then, memory forms a kind of bridge between lovers who are apart. In this song, the narrator consoles Atthis by asking her to remember that the absent woman is remembering her—"with desire" (last stanza).

The most striking feature of fragment 96 is the moon simile. The description comparing the absent woman with the moon is so protracted and so vividly painted that we almost feel transported to Lydia on a bright moonlit night—perhaps with a full moon casting its light over the sea and the dew-covered fields of flowers. The imagery is so beautiful and soothing that we almost forget the song's painful framework and the theme of separation.

Although the language of the simile is subtle, it reveals an underlying sensuality that is particularly appropriate to female eroticism. The moon (the goddess Selene to the Greeks) and the lunar cycle are traditionally connected closely to the female, as is the sea. Flowers, especially roses, are often symbols of female genitalia, and fields of any sort (here, of flowers and herbs and clover) are generally associated with female fertility. The underlying sensuality of the imagery in the moon simile, combined with the restless energy conveyed in the picture of the absent woman "roaming about far and wide" (perhaps along the seashore of the mainland, looking out towards Lesbos), vividly conveys the sense of longing and desire that is so central to this song.

THE MEMORY OF SATISFIED DESIRE: FRAGMENT 94 V.

The final love song that we will consider, fragment 94 V., was found in the same 6th century A.D. parchment as fragment 96, and is even more full of gaps. As near as we can tell, however, it presents a dialogue between an unnamed departing woman and "Sappho" (named in line 5), who seems to be reminding the other woman of all the sensual delights that they experienced together:

Fragment 94 V.

. . . .
"Honestly, I wish I were dead!"
Weeping many tears she left me,

Saying this as well:
"Oh, what dreadful things have happened to us,
Sappho! I don't want to leave you!"

I answered her:
Go with my blessings, and remember me,
for you know how we cherished you.

"But if you have [forgotten], I want

to remind you ...
of the beautiful things that happened to us:

"Close by my side you put around yourself
[many wreaths] of violets and roses and saffron....

"And many women garlands
made from flowers ...
around your tender neck,

"And ... with costly royal
myrrh ...
you anointed....

"And on a soft bed
... tender ...
you satisfied your desire ...

"Nor was there any ...
nor any holy ...
from which we were away,

... nor grove...."

Since the first line of the first three-line stanza is missing, we know that the fragment does not include the opening of the song. How much of the beginning is missing we cannot tell. The first extant line, which I have put in quotation marks on the assumption that it should be assigned to the distraught departing woman, could of course be assigned instead to the "Sappho" narrator. (Remember that the ancient copyists used no quotation marks.)

Such an interpretation used to be the prevalent one—

Sappho as the unhappy lesbian longing for death. But in more recent analyses, scholars seem to prefer to assign the first extant line to the departing woman. They point out that such a distribution of the lines makes for a more consistent internal characterization, with the departing woman exclaiming how awful the separation will be, while the "Sappho" narrator presents a calmer response, relying on the soothing effect of memory. It would not make sense for this calm "Sappho" to be expressing a death wish!

The main part of the fragment, which unfortunately trails off into complete unintelligibility at the end, consists of the narrator's memories of the past delights that the two have experienced together. Instead of the "dreadful things" that preoccupy the departing woman (the impending separation), the narrator sees only the "beautiful things that happened to us" in the past.

As in fragment 96, the poet makes use of extremely sensual imagery, speaking of wreaths and garlands of violets and roses, the anointing of bodies with fragrant myrrh, and the satisfying of desire on a soft bed. When this fragment was first published shortly after the turn of the century, one famous German classical scholar, Ulrich von Wilamowitz-Moellendorff, quickly put forward the theory that the need for "bed rest" referred to in the next-to-last stanza was doubtless owing to tiredness brought on by excessive dancing! Wilamowitz (the same scholar who proposed the wedding-song theory for fragment 31) entertained a rather fanciful notion that Sappho's "pupils" spent their days picking flowers, dancing, and learning to be proper aristocratic young ladies at Sappho's finishing school. However, since the phrase in Greek for "you satisfied your desire" in the stanza in question occurs elsewhere in Greek poetry in a clearly erotic context, Wilamowitz's Victorian interpretation seems highly unlikely.

CONCLUSION

These four fragments, despite their tattered condition, do illustrate for us the probable range of Sappho's lesbian love songs. From impassioned first-person narratives (fragment 31) to calm philosophical statements about beauty and love (fragment 16), from a song of consolation with soothing images of a moonlit night (fragment 96) to a dialogue between lovers who must part (fragment 94), we see Sappho weaving together songs of great beauty of form and powerful emotional force. They have shaped the later poetic treatment of lesbian sexuality in a measure out of all proportion to the few words of Sappho's left to us today.

SIX

What Else Did Sappho Write About?

What other woman played such a part in moulding the great literature that has moulded the world?... Modern nations must again take up the problem where Athens failed and Lesbos only pointed the way to the solution,— to create a civilization where the highest culture shall be extended to women also. It is not enough that we should dream, with Plato, of a republic where man is free and woman but a serf. The aspirations of modern life culminate, like the greatest of modern poems, in the elevation of womanhood.

—T.W. Higginson

BEFORE WE TURN IN THE FINAL chapter of this book to the subject of Sappho's influence on modern women poets, we should consider the other topics that Sappho seems to have dealt with in her poetry besides love. Although she is certainly most famous for her love poetry and her songs connected with Aphrodite, she appears to have written on a number of other themes. The present chapter gives a brief overview of what can be reconstructed from the remaining shorter fragments, many of which consist of only a line or two, or, in many cases, only a word or two.

SAPPHO'S NINE BOOKS

During the Hellenistic period (the time of Alexander the Great, who died in 323 B.C.), Greek scholars at Alexandria in Egypt collected all of Sappho's songs known to them and arranged them into nine books on the basis of meter. Ancient Greek poetry, much more so than modern poetry in English, was composed in a number of very distinctive metrical patterns based on the arrangement of short and long syllables. We know, for example, that book 1 of Sappho's poetry in the Alexandrian edition consisted of all her songs in the four-line stanza form illustrated by the "Hymn to Aphrodite" (see chapter 4), as well as by fragments 31 and 16 (see chapter 5). The total number of lines in book 1 (all in this same meter) was supposed to have been 1,320 (perhaps about 60 songs altogether). This four-line stanza form was in fact so closely identified with Sappho that it acquired the label *Sapphic stanza.*

So that you can get some idea of the rhythm of the Sapphic stanza, here is the opening line of the "Hymn to Aphrodite" with the long syllables marked – and the short syllables marked u. Hold the long syllables twice as long as the short ones (the Greek has been transliterated into our alphabet):

– u – u   – u   u   – u   – –
poi ki lo thron'   a tha nat'   A phro di to

The next two lines of the stanza follow a similar pattern, and the fourth line, which is always shorter, goes – u u – –. Now imagine a tune for the stanza (the melody would be repeated for each successive stanza) and some accompaniment provided by a sort of long-armed lyre (the *barbitos*) and you have a glimpse of Sappho's songs in action.

The final book of the Alexandrian edition, book 9, contained a miscellany of all the songs written for performance at a wedding that did not fit into earlier books on the basis of meter, so evidently the meter was not necessarily tied terribly closely to the subject matter. In other words, Sappho composed wedding songs in a variety of meters, and these songs then wound up in various of the earlier books; whatever wedding songs were left over then formed the potpourri in the final book.

The only other book whose approximate length is known is book 8, which had only about 130 lines altogether. If book 1 (1,320 lines) and book 8 are taken as extremes on either end (which they might not be, of course), then we could arrive at the figure 700 as an average length in number of lines for one of the nine books. If we multiply that figure by nine, we come up with a grand total of 6,300 lines of poetry, or perhaps roughly 300 songs, in the Alexandrian collection. When you remember that we have only one complete song left out of that number (the "Hymn to Aphrodite") and only a dozen or so fragments of any substantial length, you realize how difficult it is for us today to appreciate the range of Sappho's work. Although altogether we have roughly 200 fragments, a very large proportion of these consist of only a word or two—not enough for us to draw any conclusions at all about their context.

MYTHOLOGICAL SUBJECTS

Like nearly all ancient Greek poets, Sappho must have made use of the traditional myths in her poetry. These were the stories of the gods and goddesses and heroes first recorded by Homer in his *Iliad* and *Odyssey*. Of course, as we have already seen in the case of fragment 16 and the story of Helen (see chapter 5), Sappho sometimes cites an example from myth to prove a point in a song that is not primarily mythological in its focus. We cannot therefore just assume that a short fragment which mentions a mythological figure was necessarily a song about a given myth. For example, we have one short fragment that goes as follows:

The Archeological Record

Emmanuel-Maurice de Lorraine, who became the Duc d'Elbeuf, obtained property at Portici, where he had decided to build a villa. In the process of digging the foundation, workman unearthed priceless art, busts, and marble, from the ground which was later identified to be the site of the Theatre at Herculaneum. Unfortunately for d'Elbeuf, he was called back to his homeland and the site was later acquired by Charles of Bourbon in 1746. One of the engineers excavating the site, Karl Weber, kept exhaustive notes, helping to teach the world about the importance of the discovery. In the course of digging, many papyri were destroyed by spades and feet. A priest was sent to evaluate the site and he spotted the rolls and tried to save them. He hurried to impress their importance to the king and queen. In the later half of the 1750s, a mosaic, a painting, and a bust were all considered to be Sappho (though later they were proven wrong). The excitement over the findings spurred popular interest in the poet.

Fragment 142 V.

Leto and Niobe were very dear friends....

Niobe, a mortal woman and the wife of Amphion of Thebes, had seven sons and seven daughters. According to the myth, one day she boasted that she was superior to the goddess Leto (mother of Apollo and Artemis) in childbearing. As a consequence of this rash boast, all of her children were killed by Apollo and Artemis, and she herself was turned into a rock from which her tears of grief flowed eternally in the form of a spring. How Sappho used this story in fragment 142 we cannot tell. She might have focused on the myth itself, or she might have used the story of Niobe to illustrate how a friendship can be destroyed through arrogance.

We do have a longer fragment, however, that seems to focus entirely on a particular myth, namely the wedding of Hector and Andromache. The papyrus in which the following fragment (which is full of gaps) was preserved tells us that this piece was the last one in book 2 of the Alexandrian edition of Sappho's poems. Rather than being composed in three- or four-line stanzas like most of Sappho's verse, this poem is written in dactylic lines similar to those found in Homer's *Iliad* and *Odyssey.*

Fragment 44 V.
[The Wedding of Hector and Andromache]

Cyprus ...
The herald came,
Idaeus ... swift messenger
[who said]:
"... and of the rest of Asia ... the fame is undying.

Hector and his companions are bringing a quick-glancing
  girl
from holy Thebes and the river Plakia—
tender Andromache—in ships upon the salty
sea; many golden bracelets and purple garments
... many-colored adornments,
countless silver cups and ivory."
So he spoke. Quickly [Hector's] dear father leaped up;
the word went out over the broad-plained city to his friends.
At once the sons of Ilus yoked mules
to the well-wheeled chariots. The whole throng
of women and ... of maidens....
But apart, the daughters of Priam ...
and unmarried men yoked horses to the chariots,
and greatly ...
... charioteers ...
... like to the gods ...
... holy...
set forth ... to Ilium
and the sweet-melodied aulos [and kithara] were mingled,
and the noise of castanets.... Then the maidens
sang a holy song; the divine echo reached the sky ...
and everywhere along the road ...
libation vessels ...
myrrh and cassia and frankincense were mingled.
But the women, as many as were older, cried out,
and all the men shouted a high-pitched lovely song,
calling upon Paean, the far-shooting and well-lyred;
they sang of Hector and Andromache, like to the gods.

Despite the frequent gaps in the text, the general scheme of the
narrative is clear enough. The herald Idaeus announces the
impending arrival at Troy of Hector, crown prince of Troy and

the son of Priam (king of Troy), together with his bride Andromache. They are accompanied by many wedding gifts (silver
cups and so forth). Priam passes the word on to the rest of the
city, and all the men of Troy get horses and chariots ready while
the young girls sing to the music of the aulos (an oboelike
instrument), kithara (similar to a lyre), and castanets. Libations
and incense are prepared, and everyone sings to Apollo (here
called Paean) in praise of the bride and groom. Scholars have
suggested that perhaps fragment 44 was written to be performed at a real wedding on Lesbos, but we have no way of
knowing for sure.

WEDDINGS AND OTHER RITUALS

Several of the shorter fragments of Sappho's poetry very
clearly belong to the genre of the wedding song, or what the
Greeks called the hymeneal. (We have later examples of the
genre, so we can recognize its characteristics.) The Greeks
thought of their *hymeneals* as being in honor of the god of
marriage, Hymen. Although some of the following fragments
display a certain poignancy at the thought of the bride's passage from girlhood into maturity, most of them seem to be
lighthearted in tone, sometimes with mocking allusions to the
size of the groom (comparing him to Ares, the god of war) or
to the size of the doorkeeper's feet:

Fragment 111 V.

Raise high the roofbeams!
Sing the Hymeneal!
Raise it high, O carpenter men!
Sing the Hymeneal!
The bridegroom enters, like to Ares,
by far bigger than a big man.

Fragment 110a V.
[At the wedding]

the doorkeeper's feet are seven fathoms long,
and his sandals are made of five ox hides,
and ten shoemakers worked away to make them.

Fragment 113 V.

Bridegroom, never will there be another girl like this!

Fragment 105a V.
[the bride]

just like a sweet apple which ripens on the uppermost
    bough,
on the top of the topmost; but the apple gatherers forgot it,
or rather, they didn't forget it, but they could not reach
it....

Fragment 114 V.

Bride: Maidenhood, maidenhood, where have you gone and
left me?
Maidenhood: No more will I come back to you, no more
will I come back.

Particularly touching among the examples just given is fragment 105a, in which the bride is compared to a beautiful apple
so high up on the apple tree that the pickers couldn't quite
reach the object of their pursuit. Thus the apple escapes their
hands and is allowed to ripen fully, still in its place on the topmost bough.

Other short fragments among those we have left seem to allude to rituals other than wedding ceremonies. In the following example, Sappho appears to describe a moonlit ritual involving a sacred altar:

Fragment 154 V.

The moon gleamed in its fullness,
and as the women stood around the altar....

And in this next fragment, she seems to be describing some kind of ceremony in which a woman called Dika is instructed to weave garlands of flowers into her hair in order to be more pleasing to the Graces, the three daughters of Zeus who represent beauty and loveliness:

Fragment 81b V.

O Dika, put lovely garlands on your tresses,
binding together shoots of dill in your tender hands.
For the blessed Graces favor more the well-flowered,
but turn away the ungarlanded.

FAMILY AND FRIENDS

Although it must be stressed again that lack of context prevents certainty about the subject matter of many of the shorter fragments, the following are examples that may have been parts of songs about a family member or a friend. Fragment 5 V., which may be addressed to Aphrodite (the Cyprian) as well as the Nereids (sea nymphs who can protect sailors), is a prayer for the safety of the narrator's brother. Scholars have surmised that the poem may be about Sappho's brother Charaxus (see chapter 2), who (Herodotus informs us) had business enterprises in Egypt and thus no doubt had to go on dangerous sea voyages with some frequency. Like the "Hymn to Aphrodite," this prayer for the brother's safety is written in four-line Sapphic stanzas:

Fragment 5 V.

O [Cyprian] and Nereids, grant
that my brother come hither unharmed
and that as many things as he wishes in his heart to come
   about
are all brought to pass,

And that he atones for all his former errors,
and is a joy to his [friends],
a [pain] to his enemies; but for us
let there be no misery.
May he wish to do honor to his sister
... painful suffering ... of the citizens ...
... Cyprian ...

Several of the shorter fragments seem to be concerned with Sappho's friends, although without the context we cannot always be sure that the lines were not part of a love song. Here is one especially tantalizing bit (preserved through quotation by a later writer) that seems to be the beginning of a programmatic statement of Sappho's poetic mission:

Fragment 160 V.

Now I will sing beautifully
to delight my women companions....

In this case, at least, Sappho seems to be directing her songs at a female audience composed of her companions (*hetairai*, but without the Athenian sense of "prostitute" as discussed above in chapter 3).

The following two fragments both appear to praise women for their wisdom or beauty:

Fragment 56 V.

I do not think there will be at any time
a woman who looks on the light of the sun
with wisdom such as yours....

Fragment 156 V.

[A woman] far more sweet-melodied than a harp,
more golden than gold ...

BEAUTY

Beauty is, in fact, a subject that seems to concern Sappho in a number of the shorter fragments. No doubt the following fragments formed part of various kinds of songs, but they illustrate a recurring delight that Sappho expresses over both natural beauty (e.g., of the moon) and beautiful handwrought goods. Only in one of them (fragment 98b V.) does the darker side of life seem to intrude—in the form of an apparent allusion to political turmoil and consequent exile of one of the rival clans:

Fragment 98b V.

For you, Kleis, I have no
many-colored headband, nor

do I know where one will come from.
But for the Mytilenean ...
... these memories of the exile
of the sons of Kleanax ...
... for they wasted away terribly ...

Fragment 98a V.

... for my mother [said that]
in her youth it was indeed a great ornament if someone had
   tresses
wrapped in a purple [band].
But the girl who has hair
brighter than a fiery torch
should wear [?] wreaths
of blooming flowers.
Just now a many-colored
headband from Sardis ...

Fragment 39 V.

But a many-colored thong
concealed her feet—a beautiful
Lydian work.

Fragment 43 V.

The stars around the beautiful moon
keep hidden their glittering radiance,
whenever in its fullness it shines
[upon] the earth.

RIVALS

Several of the shorter fragments seem to refer to women whom Sappho considers unworthy of the standards that she herself holds to. Whether these were personal standards or standards of beauty or poetic standards is anyone's guess. The following fragment, for example, sounds like a criticism of someone of inferior poetic mettle, to judge from the allusion to the "roses of Pieria"; Pieria was the home of the Muses, so Sappho seems to be predicting that this uninspired woman will be doomed to eternal obscurity:

Fragment 55 V.

You will lie dead, nor will there be anyone
remembering you later; for you have no share\
in the roses of Pieria, but will roam unseen
in the house of Hades, having flown off among dim corpses.

Another fragment displays Sappho's caustic wit as she puns on the name of a woman whom she seems only too happy to bid good-bye to:

Fragment 155 V.

I'm overjoyed to say farewell to you, Miss Overlord.

Envy of a rival is perhaps suggested in this brief snippet, in which the woman named Atthis may be the same individual addressed in fragment 96 (see chapter 5):

Fragment 131 V.

At this, it has become hateful to you to think
of me; but you fly instead to Andromeda.

Whatever lies behind these hints of disapproval or envy, Sappho's estimation of her own self-worth as a writer is unequivocal. She predicts her own lasting reputation as a lyric poet:

Fragment 147 V.

I say that even later someone will remember us.

EROS

Although in all likelihood Sappho did write about myths, weddings, family and friends, beauty, and inferior poets, it is clear that the subject of love and of erotic pursuits was her chief concern. Certainly her reputation in ancient times was based firmly on her erotic verse. Her concern with the erotic is revealed as well in the shorter fragments that deal (directly or indirectly) with Eros, the god of love, whom the Greeks thought of as a primeval force who came into being at the early stages of creation.

For Sappho, Eros is both a creative force (in that he provides the subject matter for so many of her songs) and a destructive force (in that his power over mere mortals is sometimes completely overwhelming and confusing):

Fragment 188 V.

Eros, weaver of stories ...

Fragment 47 V.

Eros shook my heart, like the wind
assailing the oaks on a mountain.

Fragment 130 V.

Eros the loosener of limbs shakes me again
bittersweet, untamable, crawling creature.

Fragment 51 V.

I do not know what to do; my mind is split.

Fragment 102 V.

Sweet mother, I am not able to weave at my loom,
overwhelmed with desire for a youth because of tender
   Aphrodite.

A few of the fragments, to be sure, do suggest a calmer side of
Eros and erotic desire, but we must again remember that we are
dealing with very partial excerpts of whole songs. It is hard to
say how we might interpret the following lines if we had their
surrounding contexts:

Fragment 49 V.

I loved you, Atthis, once long ago....
You seemed to me to be a small and graceless child.

Fragment 48 V.

You came, you did [well?], and I wanted you;
you made cool my heart, which was burning with desire.

Fragment 121 V.

But since you are our friend,
seek a younger bed.
For I would not dare
to live with you, since I am older.

Fragment 126 V.

May you sleep in the bosom of a tender woman friend.

CONCLUSION

On the basis of the one complete song that we have left, the more substantial fragments presented in chapters 4 and 5, and the sampling of the shorter fragments studied in this chapter, it is hard not to agree with the assessment of a well-known modern American writer, Willa Cather, who greatly admired Sappho's poetry: "If of all the lost richness we could have one master restored to us, one of all the philosophers and poets, the choice of the world would be for the lost nine books of Sappho."

seven

Sappho as an Inspiration for 20th-Century Women Writers

you were already
a speaking instrument
I loved the speaker
loved the voice
as it broke my heart with pity
                    —Carolyn Kizer, "For Sappho/After Sappho"

IF THERE IS ONE MOTIF that seems to be a particularly distinctive mark of poetry written by lesbian women in the 20th century, it is the motif of isolation. Although the works of Amy Lowell, Renée Vivien, Hilda Doolittle, May Sarton, and Olga Broumas are disparate in style and theme, they do share in common a sense of separateness and difference. Sappho and her homeland of Lesbos have provided these and other modern women poets with a convenient metaphor for this isolation. Sappho floats across the centuries as an island in the sea of writers of the past, a solitary example of a woman writer attempting to define woman's desire for woman. Lesbos becomes a symbol of the lost past, an isolated place that must be re-created through the archaeology of words. I hope that the few examples of modern women poets that I have chosen for this chapter will suggest the richness of Sappho's legacy to 20th-century literature, whether direct or indirect. Some of these poets studied Sappho's poems in the original ancient Greek (Renée Vivien and Hilda Doolittle), while others probably read them only in modern translation, but all of them follow in Sappho's footsteps as celebrators of female desire.

AMY LOWELL, 1874–1925

Amy Lowell was a prolific poet who was born in 1874 into Boston's distinguished Lowell dynasty. Her father, Augustus Lowell, was a wealthy businessman, and her oldest brother, Percival, established what is now the famous Lowell Observatory in Flagstaff, Arizona. Another brother, Abbott Lawrence Lowell, became president of Harvard. After her father's death in 1900, Amy Lowell inherited Sevenels, the family manor in Brookline, Massachusetts (so named because it once housed seven Lowells or *L*s) along with an income that enabled her to pursue to the fullest her interests in travel, theater, gardening, and writing. Although in her youth she was denied the formal education that her brothers received, she was well-read and well prepared for the literary enterprises that soon became her chief preoccupation. Eccentric in appearance and work habits (she was extremely stout, and she preferred to write at night and sleep during the day), she shocked Boston society with her penchant for smoking large black cigars.

By 1915, Lowell had invited an actress named Ada Dwyer to join her at Sevenels. Although their lesbian relationship is still denied by a few modern scholars, it seems clear that Dwyer became for Lowell what Alice B. Toklas was for Gertrude Stein: companion, confidante, muse, manager, and lover. When Lowell died in 1925, Ada Dwyer inherited Sevenels and an ample fortune.

Today Lowell is remembered for her identification with the movement of modernist poetry that Ezra Pound labeled Imagism, whose chief exponents, along with Pound and Lowell, were the American poets Hilda Doolittle (H.D.) and William Carlos Williams, and the English poet Richard Aldington. Their aim was to write short, direct poems that focus on a concrete image, using ordinary language and creating new rhythms rather than relying on the conventional metrical forms of Western literature. Deeply influenced by the Japanese verse form called haiku, Lowell fostered the Imagist movement, promoting her own and others' poems in a three-volume anthology entitled *Some Imagist Poets*, as well as lecturing frequently and with great enthusiasm on contemporary poetry. In her own day, Lowell's reputation was greater than that of Pound and the other Imagists. But literary history as written by the male academics after World War II effectively eradicated Lowell's name from the historical record, a fate common to many women artists and writers until feminist criticism in the 1970s revived their reputations.

In one of Lowell's own contemplative, non-Imagist poems

entitled "The Sisters," she muses on the subject of her literary predecessors, including Sappho, Elizabeth Barrett Browning, and Emily Dickinson. Lowell imagines herself as a member of a strange little family of writing women, with whom she wishes she might converse. Too lengthy to quote in its entirety, the poem opens with an introduction about the rarity of women poets and turns quickly to praise of Sappho:

> Taking us by and large, we're a queer lot
> We women who write poetry. And when you think
> How few of us there've been, it's queerer still.
> I wonder what it is that makes us do it,
> Singles us out to scribble down, man-wise,
> The fragments of ourselves. Why are we
> Already mother-creatures, double-bearing,
> With matrices in body and in brain?
> I rather think that there is just the reason
> We are so sparse a kind of human being;
> The strength of forty thousand Atlases
> Is needed for our every-day concerns.
> There's Sapho [sic], now I wonder what was Sapho.
> I know a single slender thing about her:
> That, loving, she was like a burning birch-tree
> All tall and glittering fire, and that she wrote
> Like the same fire caught up to Heaven and held there,
> A frozen blaze before it broke and fell.
> Ah, me! I wish I could have talked to Sapho,
> Surprised her reticences by flinging mine
> Into the wind. This tossing off of garments
> Which cloud the soul is none too easy doing
> With us to-day. But still I think with Sapho
> One might accomplish it, were she in the mood
> To bare her loveliness of words and tell

The reasons, as she possibly conceived them
Of why they are so lovely. Just to know
How she came at them, just to watch
The crisp sea sunshine playing on her hair
And listen, thinking all the while 'twas she
Who spoke and that we two were sisters
Of a strange, isolated little family.

Sappho's poetry was attractive to Lowell and the other Imagists, no doubt partly because in their fragmentary state, many of the pieces of her verse focus on a single vivid image—the moon shining over the sea and the fields, or the temple shaded by boughs of apple trees. In her love lyrics, Lowell adopts Sappho's personal voice in poems that are addressed directly to the figure of the lover.

Since Lowell published such a large quantity of poetry, in a brief survey such as this I can quote only a few examples to illustrate Lowell's affinity to Sappho's love poetry. Consider this unabashed celebration of the narrator's feelings of desire for an unnamed beautiful addressee (female, we assume), whose physical presence is conveyed through images of lilies, sunlight, birds, jonquils, and other elements of nature:

In Excelsis

You—you—
Your shadow is sunlight on a plate of silver;
Your footsteps, the seeding-place of lilies;
Your hands moving, a chime of bells across a windless air.

The movement of your hands is the long,
Golden running of light from a rising sun;
It is the hopping of birds upon a garden-path.

As the perfume of jonquils, you come forth in the morning.
Young horses are not more sudden than your thoughts,
Your words are bees about a pear-tree,
Your fancies are the gold-and-black striped wasps buzzing
    among red apples.
I drink your lips,
I eat the whiteness of your hands and feet.
My mouth is open,
As a new jar I am empty and open.
Like white water are you who fill the cup of my mouth,
Like a brook of water thronged with lilies.

You are frozen as the clouds,
You are far and sweet as the high clouds.
I dare to reach to you,
I dare touch the rim of your brightness.
I leap beyond the winds,
I cry and shout,
For my throat is keen as a sword
Sharpened on a hone of ivory.
My throat sings the joy of my eyes,
The rushing gladness of my love.

How has the rainbow fallen upon my heart?
How have I snared the seas to lie in my fingers
And caught the sky to be a cover for my head?
How have you come to dwell with me,
Compassing me with the four circles of your mystic light
    ness,
So that I say "Glory! Glory!" and bow before you
As to a shrine?

Do I tease myself that morning is morning and a day after?

Do I think the air a condescension,
The earth a politeness,
Heaven a boon deserving thanks?
So you—air—earth—heaven—
I do not thank you,
I take you,
I live.
And those things which I say in consequence
Are rubies mortised in a gate of stone.

The motif of the lover as a vessel to be filled up recurs in the
next short piece on the theme of lovers' separation, which, like
Sappho's fragment 96, presents us with images of moonlight
and flowers:

Absence

My cup is empty to-night,
Cold and dry are its sides,
Chilled by the wind from the open window.
Empty and void, it sparkles white in the moonlight.
The room is filled with the strange scent
Of wistaria blossoms.
They sway in the moon's radiance
And tap against the wall.
But the cup of my heart is still,
And cold, and empty.
When you come, it brims
Red and trembling with blood,
Heart's blood for your drinking;
To fill your mouth with love
And the bitter-sweet taste of a soul.

In this last example, the narrator's words themselves become vessels for the beloved to take. From the little word jars emanate sweet scents of flowers:

A Gift

See! I give myself to you, Beloved!
My words are little jars
For you to take and put upon a shelf.
Their shapes are quaint and beautiful,
And they have many pleasant colours and lustres
To recommend them.
Also the scent from them fills the room
With sweetness of flowers and crushed grasses.

When I shall have given you the last one,
You will have the whole of me,
But I shall be dead.

RENEE VIVIEN, 1877–1909

Renée Vivien, whose birth name was Pauline Tarn, was born into a wealthy family in London in 1877 of an American mother and an English father. Vivien was sent as a student to Paris, where she fell in love with a young American woman named Violet Shilleto. The relationship was intense but platonic, and after her family called her back to England so that she could prepare for her proper place in society, she rebelled against their plans for her and returned to her life in Paris. Through Shilleto she met another American, Natalie Barney (from Dayton and Cincinnati, Ohio), with whom she had her first sexual relationship.

Vivien and Barney continued their relationship from 1899 to 1901, with a brief resumption in 1904. Tortured as the relationship seems to have been for Vivien, who was unable to accept Barney's constant pursuit of other women, it had an enormous influence on Vivien's writing. As part of their joint effort to create a community in which women were liberated from the conventional expectations of society and in which homosexuality was accepted, Vivien decided to learn classical Greek so that she could study Sappho in the original language. She and Barney saw themselves as latter-day Greeks and even traveled to Lesbos in 1904 in pursuit of their spiritual ancestors.

By the time Vivien died of pneumonia in 1909 at the early age of 32 (the result of excessive drinking and anorexia during her final years), she had produced some 20 volumes containing poetry, short stories, an autobiographical novel called *Une femme m'apparut* (*A Woman Appeared to Me*), and a biography of Anne Boleyn, the second wife of Henry VIII.

All of Vivien's works were written in her adopted language, French. In addition to her own original poetry dealing openly with love between women, she translated the fragments of Sappho and other ancient women writers into French in the hopes of making their work accessible to the public. Indeed, Sappho was the central element in Vivien's aesthetic vision. As the character in Vivien's autobiographical novel who was modeled on Barney (called Vally) puts it,

"One can't imagine how to celebrate in literature what is unesthetic," Vally agreed, "and men are The Unesthetic par excellence. If there are only a few women writers and poets, it is because women are too often forced by convention to write about men. That is enough to paralyze any effort toward Beauty. Thus the only woman poet whose immortality equals that of statues is Psappha [Sappho], who didn't deign to notice masculine existence. She celebrated the sweet speech and the adorable smile of At this, and not the muscled torso of the imaginary Phaon."

Not until some 70 years after her death did some of Vivien's French poems begin to appear as translations into her native language, English. The pervasive influence of Sappho is apparent even just in the titles of some of these pieces: "Toward Lesbos," "Landing at Mytilene," "Sappho Lives Again," and "Come, Goddess of Kupros [Aphrodite]." Here is an excerpt from a poem titled "Like This Would I Speak," in which Vivien not only echoes the imagery of Sappho's songs (roses, cushions, nectar, etc.) but also creates a Sappho figure who becomes a goddesslike character in the narrative:

> I will go far from your flock of chaste believers,
> Remembering, along the paths of the wild daffodils,
>
> And there, talking of love to the one that I see
> So blond, who long charmed my ravished eyes.
>
> I would learn that lilies are more lovely than roses,
> And that song has less sense of infinity than the pauses ...
>
> Our eyes still filled with a sun long dead,
> We will contemplate our burning past.
>
> Sappho, her restless fingers on the sleeping lyre,
> Will marvel at the beauty of my lover,
>
> And the maiden of my desire, like the lily,
> Will seem to her more graceful and supple than Atthis.

Sappho will shower us, in her fervent breath,
With the odes whose melodies charmed Mytilene.

And we will prepare the flowers and the flames,
We who have loved her in a century less beautiful.

Sappho will serve us, amid the gold and silk
Of soft cushions, nectar mixed with joy.

She will show us, in her graceful manner,
The Lesbian orchard that opens to the sea.

The sweet orchard, ringing with cicadas, where
The scent of the vine trails off, vibrant as a voice.

HILDA DOOLITTLE (H.D.), 1886–1961

Hilda Doolittle, or H.D., as she became known, was born in Bethlehem, Pennsylvania, in 1886 and attended Bryn Mawr College. The daughter of a professor of astronomy and a former teacher of art and music, she was once engaged to the poet Ezra Pound, but married a friend of Pound's, the English poet Richard Aldington, in 1913. She also had a close friendship with D.H. Lawrence, whom she first met during the same year that she met Amy Lowell (1914). Shortly after the birth of her daughter, Frances Perdita (the name of whose father she never revealed) in 1919, she and Aldington separated, although they did not obtain a divorce until 1938. A prolific poet for most of her life, H.D. died in Switzerland in 1961, having been the first woman ever to receive, the year before her death, the American Academy of Arts and Letters Award of Merit for poetry.

Like her nationality (although born in America, she spent most of her life in England and elsewhere in Europe), her sexuality is not easy to categorize. Apparently bisexual in inclination, H.D. had a youthful love affair with Frances Gregg (after whom she named her daughter), and spent much of her life from 1920 on in the company of a wealthy writer named Winifred Ellerman, who preferred to be known simply by the name Bryher. Although Bryher, the daughter of a British shipping magnate, married twice, both were marriages of convenience that were never consummated.

Bryher assisted H.D. in a number of ways, including helping to raise and support H.D.'s daughter (whom she legally adopted), as well as sponsoring joint trips to Greece, America, and Egypt, not to mention paying for H.D. to be analyzed by Freud in Vienna in 1933 and 1934. Theirs was a complex relationship that eludes easy definition, but it clearly had lesbian aspects. Evidently it was somewhat one-sided, in that Bryher was completely devoted to H.D., while H.D. insisted on maintaining at least a limited form of independence despite her reliance on Bryher in caring for Perdita.

Although a few of H.D.'s poems are still regularly anthologized, particularly her early Imagist poems, her later, more fully developed poems and her homoerotic novels are only rarely studied today, perhaps partly because she chose to focus on women as subjects. Much of her poetry also demands a knowledge of Greek mythology, for she was deeply drawn to the stories of Greek epic and tragedy, which she alludes to frequently in her verse. As a young woman she had studied both Greek and Latin, and her familiarity with Greek and Roman literature had a profound influence on her writing.

It is impossible to do justice to so complex a poet in a brief survey such as this, but a few examples of H.D.'s shorter pieces will illustrate her connections with Sappho. Her fascination with the fragments of Sappho's poetry is revealed explicitly in a short essay (not published until after her death) entitled "The Wise Sappho." Speaking of the colors red, scarlet, and gold, she says, "I think of the words of Sappho as these colours, or states rather, transcending colour yet containing (as great heat the compass of the spectrum) all colour. And perhaps the most obvious is this rose colour, merging to richer shades of scarlet, purple or Phoenician purple."

In 1924, H.D. published a collection of poems called *Heliodora*, which included several pieces very loosely based on some of Sappho's shorter fragments. One was derived from Sappho fragment 51 V., which translates, "I do not know what to do; my mind is split." H.D. expands the fragment into a wrenching statement of divided attention on the part of the speaker, who apparently feels torn between her devotion to her art as a poet and her passion for the unnamed you of the second stanza (the edition of Sappho that H.D. used had a different numbering system from that used today, so her titles do not correspond to the fragment numbers in the present book). Here are the poem's opening stanzas:

Fragment 36

I know not what to do:
my mind is divided.—Sappho

I know not what to do,
my mind is reft:
is song's gift best?
is love's gift loveliest?
I know not what to do,
now sleep has pressed
weight on your eyelids.

Shall I break your rest,
devouring, eager?

is love's gift best?
nay, song's the loveliest:
yet were you lost,
what rapture
could I take from song?
what song were left?

I know not what to do:
to turn and slake
the rage that burns,
with my breath burn
and trouble your cool breath?
so shall I turn and take
snow in my arms?
(is love's gift best?)
yet flake on flake
of snow were comfortless,
did you lie wondering,
wakened yet unawake.

Many of H.D.'s shorter poems are reminiscent of Sappho in the choice of imagery, which often includes references to violets and myrrh and purple hyacinths, not to mention moonlight and the sea. Here is one example, a lovely piece addressed to the moon in the collective person of women who seem to be followers of the huntress Artemis (Diana), a deity who was closely identified with the moon and with female fertility:

Moonrise

Will you glimmer on the sea?
will you fling your spear-head
on the shore?

what note shall we pitch?
we have a song,
on the bank we share our arrows;
the loosed string tells our note:
O flight
bring her swiftly to our song.
She is great,
we measure her by the pine trees.

MAY SARTON, B. 1912

May Sarton was born Eleanor Marie Sarton in 1912 in Belgium. When she was still a small child, her parents, George and

Lesbianism as Pulp Fiction

Sappho made an appearance in grocery stores, as part of popular lesbian pulp fiction of the 1950s and '60s. The 'Sapphic' tales often told of an older, sexually aggressive woman who preyed on younger women. Inevitably, after pages of titillation, the woman would suffer some sort of comeuppance for her deviant ways. This retribution kept the books from being considered mere pornography as they offered a moral lesson to readers. According to an article by Maureen McClamon of the Sallie Bingham Center for Women's History and Culture, the luridly covered books were coded. Lesbian titles often included the words 'strange', 'odd', or 'shadows'. Although intended for a heterosexual audience, the books found a core market with women, particularly lesbians who were looking for at least some mention of their lives. With the growing power of the Gay and Lesbian Movement, the books fell out of favor, but not before providing a training ground for beginning writers like Marion Zimmer Bradley (*The Mists of Avalon* author) who wrote under pseudonyms (*scriptorium.lib.duke.edu/women/pulp.html*).

Mabel Sarton, immigrated to the United States and settled in Cambridge, Massachusetts. There George Sarton became a distinguished professor of the history of science at Harvard University. May Sarton graduated from Cambridge High and Latin School in 1929, and after several years of experience in theater, turned her attention exclusively to publishing poetry, novels, and memoirs. The recipient of a Guggenheim Award in 1955, she has served as writer-in-residence at a number of American colleges and is the author of a long list of volumes of poetry, 14 novels, several fables and works for children, as well as a series of personal journals recording her life as a woman and an artist.

Sarton's novel *Mrs. Stevens Hears the Mermaids Singing*, published in 1965, was an unusually bold appraisal (for its time) of the homoerotic sources of inspiration for the protagonist, a woman writer whose life bears a certain resemblance to Sarton's own. Sarton lived for many years in Cambridge, Massachusetts, with Judith Matlack, to whom she refers in the journals simply as Judy. Here is a poem that she mentions—long after its original publication—had been written for her companion in tribute to their shared domestic life:

A Light Left On

In the evening we came back
Into our yellow room,
For a moment taken aback
To find the light left on,
Falling on silent flowers,
Table, book, empty chair
While we had gone elsewhere,
Had been away for hours.

When we came home together
We found the inside weather.
All of our love unended
The quiet light demanded,
And we gave, in a look
At yellow walls and open book.
The deepest world we share
And do not talk about
But have to have, was there,
And by that light found out.

In 1958, Sarton left the town of her childhood for Nelson, New Hampshire, and moved again in 1973, this time to a house by the sea in York, Maine, where she has lived alone for the past two decades. Although she has suffered poor health in recent years, she has continued producing journals, and it is primarily to these memoirs that she owes her fame as an advocate of solitude and a champion of female creativity, whether in gardening or the writing of poetry.

As a poet, May Sarton is the most conventional of the writers discussed in this chapter, often preferring traditional rhyme schemes such as the 14-line sonnet. Unlike Amy Lowell or H.D., she could not be described as an experimental poet, and indeed, she prides herself on her technical mastery of existing poetic forms. Her verse is both formal and reserved, and without the aid of her journals and recent interviews with her, a reader might not even notice the lesbian framework of her love poetry. Her subjects are varied, ranging (in addition to the love poems) from responses to works of art to comments on the natural world to poems inspired by her many travels.

May Sarton's verse reflects Sapphic sensibilities more than it does any direct influence of Sappho. She does mention the ancient poet's name, along with Emily Dickinson and Christina

Rossetti, in a poem called "My Sisters, O My Sisters," but unlike H.D., she has written no poems that actually use one of Sappho's fragments as a point of takeoff. However, she did visit Greece as part of her 50th birthday celebration, and at the end of the second section of the following poem (quoted here in part), we note what is perhaps an echo of Sappho fragment 51 V. ("I do not know what to do; my mind is split"):

Birthday on the Acropolis

1
In the fifth grade
We became Greeks,
Made our own chitons,
Drank homemade mead,
and carved a small Parthenon
Out of Ivory soap.
It never seemed real,
The substance too soft,
An awkward miniature.

. . .

2
Forty years later
I was hurled to the bright rock,
Still merged with the dark,
Edgeless and melting,
The Indian ethos—
Stepped out from the plane
To stand in the Greek light
In the knife-clean air.

Too sudden, too brilliant.
Who can bear this shining?
The pitiless clarity?
Each bone felt the shock.
I was broken in two
by sheer definition:

Rock, light, air....

Like Sappho, Sarton speaks of Aphrodite's encounters with us
mortals, although her portrait of the goddess seems as much
influenced by Botticelli's *Birth of Venus* as by the ancient poet:

The Return of Aphrodite

Under the wave it is altogether still,
Alive and still, as nourishing as sleep,
Down below conflict, beyond need or will,
Where love flows on and yet is there to keep,
As unconstrained as waves that lift and break
And their bright foam neither to give nor take.

Listen to the long rising curve and stress,
Murmur of ocean that brings us the goddess.

From deep she rises, poised upon her shell.
Oh guiltless Aphrodite so long absent!
The green waves part. There is no sound at all
As she advances, tranquil and transparent,
To lay on mortal flesh her sacred mantle.

The wave recedes—she is drawn back again
Into the ocean where light leaves a stain.

The following poem, perhaps also the fruit of Sarton's visit to Greece, suggests the same tranquillity of place that Sappho conveys in her description of Aphrodite's sacred precinct (Sappho frag. 2 V):

Mediterranean

Here is the ample place,
Hid in the sacred wood,
Where the intense young face
Meets the calm antique god.

Light flowing through the vine
Where air and earth are one;
Here are the sovereign wine,
The dark bread, the gold sun.

Distill all that's concrete
And make of it a prayer:
Air is the fig you eat;
The wine you drink is air.

This is the calm god's will,
And what he knows you know.
Lie under the terraced wall
And let the anguish go.

Let fall the torturing dream
Where the slow oxen move.
All things are what they seem
Here in the sacred grove.

Finally, the theme of separation and loss that is so poignantly treated by Sappho's literary descendants finds expression as well in this stanza from "A Divorce of Lovers," written in Shakespearean sonnet form:

I shall not see the end of this unweaving.
I shall lie dead in any narrow ditch
Before they are unwoven, love and grieving,
And our lives separated stitch by stitch.
I shall be dead before this task is done,
Not for a moment give you your cool head.
Say we had twenty years and now have none—
Are you Old Fate itself to snap the thread,
And to cut both your life and mine in half
Before the whole design is written clear?
This tapestry will not unweave itself,
Nor I spend what is left of me to tear
Your bright thread out: let unfilled design
Stand as your tragic epitaph, and mine.

OLGA BROUMAS, b. 1949

Like Sappho, Olga Broumas was born (in 1949) on a Greek island—not Lesbos, but Syros, one of the Cyclades islands in the middle of the Aegean Sea. The daughter of a Greek army officer, she lived in Washington, D.C., for two years as a child before coming to the United States permanently in 1967. In 1977, she was chosen as the 72nd winner of the Yale Series of Younger Poets competition, an award that solidified her already promising reputation as a poet despite what might have been the handicap of writing in an adopted language. She is the recipient of degrees in architecture and creative writing, and has won fellowships from the National Endowment for the Arts and the Guggenheim Foundation in support of her writing. In addition to being a poet, she is also a massage therapist and a teacher of creative writing.

Of all the poets considered in this brief survey, Broumas is the most forthright in her celebration of female sexuality and lesbian desire. She draws heavily upon classical Greek mythology in her poetry, portraying an all-female world in which she herself becomes a kind of modern Sappho. Like Sappho, she transforms the ancient myths for her own purposes, even going so far as to change the gender, for example, of Leda's swan from male to female; what had been a story of the rape of Leda by Zeus (as the swan) becomes instead a celebration of the lovemaking of two women, as "amaryllis blooms / in your upper thighs, water lily / on mine ..." (from "Leda and Her Swan").

One of Broumas' poems ("Bitterness") is preceded by an epigraph attributed to Sappho:

She who loves roses must be patient
and not cry out when she is pierced by thorns.

In the explanatory notes for this particular poem, however, Broumas confesses that she found these lines in the midst of a page of her own notes on Sappho, and, not being able to locate them among Sappho's fragments, wonders if she didn't write them herself under Sappho's influence. Such must have indeed been the case, for the lines are not Sappho's. In any case, Broumas's indebtedness to her ancient predecessor is plain to see.

In another poem ("Demeter") she also associates herself closely with four 20th-century literary foremothers, whom she calls "Anne. Sylvia. Virginia. / Adrienne the last, magnificent last," referring to Anne Sexton, Sylvia Plath, Virginia Woolf, and Adrienne Rich. Of these, Rich has been writing explicitly lesbian love poetry over the past two decades, thus offering to Broumas (along with Sappho and the women writers whom she names) a much fuller tradition than was available to Amy Lowell as she searched for connections with other writing women at the beginning of the 20th century. Although the motif of the island still recurs in Broumas's poetry, of all the poets considered in this chapter, she seems to express the smallest degree of isolation.

Broumas does, however, speak of the "archaeology of an excised past" (in "Artemis"), referring to the need to find new meanings of words to express the lost history of the female body. In the same poem, she goes on (in the persona of the goddess Artemis) to proclaim:

> I work
> in silver the tongue-like forms
> that curve round a throat
>
> an arm-pit, the upper
> thigh, whose significance stirs in me
> like a curviform alphabet
> that defies
>
> decoding, appears
> to consist of vowels, beginning with O, the O-
> mega, horseshoe, the cave of sound.
> What tiny fragments
>
> survive, mangled into our language.

This is the title piece for the collection in which it appears (*Beginning with O*). The female body is here identified with an alphabet, the most basic element of language, an alphabet that begins with omega. When we remember that omega is in fact the last letter of the Greek alphabet (as in the expression "from alpha to omega," meaning from beginning to end), we see the extent of the revolutionary nature of Broumas's undertaking. The omega, which Broumas calls the "cave of sound," clearly suggests the interiority of the female body and its harboring recesses. Broumas seeks a whole new language that will encompass what has been left out over the centuries, what is discernible only through digging and decoding—the body of woman as subject, not merely as object.

The celebration of lesbian desire and erotic action becomes for Broumas a theme of defiant insistence on acceptance by the broader culture. Unlike Sappho, who seems utterly unselfconscious about the nature of the desire that she defines, Broumas is confidently aware of the boldness of her action in reclaiming the excised past and in proclaiming a desire excluded by patriarchal norms. In the last section of a poem called "Sleeping Beauty," she offers this vignette of the physical closeness of two women in the face of public awareness:

> City-center, mid-
> traffic, I
> wake to your public kiss. Your name
> is Judith, your kiss a sign
>
> to the shocked pedestrians, gathered
> beneath the light that means
> stop
> in our culture
> where red is a warning, and men
> threaten each other with final violence: *I will drink
> your blood.* Your kiss
> is for them

a sign of betrayal, your red
lips suspect, unspeakable
liberties as
we cross the street, kissing
against the light, singing, This
is the woman I woke from sleep, the woman that woke
me sleeping.

Echoes of Sappho drifting up from the distant past are so frequent in Broumas's poems that it is difficult to single out
individual examples. Nevertheless, perhaps the following
poem entitled "Thetis" (after the sea nymph who dwelled in
the waves with her 49 sisters, the Nereids) is as good an
example as any of the sense of female community and female
bonding common to both authors. In a context of images
reminiscent of Sappho's association of women with the sea
and moonlight, the narrator Thetis describes a safe female
space and advises the addressee on how to protect herself from
unwanted male invasion and impregnation:

Thetis

No. I'm not tired, the tide
is late tonight, go
with your sisters, go
sleep, go play.
No? Then come
closer, sit here, look

where we strung the fruit, hammocks of
apples, dates, orange peel. Look
at the moon

lolling between them, indolent
as a suckled breast. Do you understand

child, how the moon, the tide
is our own
image? Inland
the women call themselves *Tidal Pool*
call their water jars Women, insert
sponge and seaweed
under each curly, triangular thatch. Well

there's the salt lip, finally
drawing back. You must understand
everything that caresses you
will not be like this
moon-bright water, pleasurable, fertile
only with mollusks and fish. There are still
other fluids, fecund, tail-whipped
with seed. There are ways to evade them. Go
get a strand

of kelp. Fold it, down in your palm
like a cup, a hood. Good.
Squat down beside me.
Facing the moon.

CONCLUSION

Amy Lowell, Renée Vivien, H.D., May Sarton, and Olga
Broumas are only a few of the women poets of this century who
might have been discussed in connection with the legacy of
Sappho. Clearly, their successors in the 21st century will have a
wealth of tradition upon which to build. The "strange, isolated
little family" that Amy Lowell envisioned may still be regarded

in some quarters as strange, but it is no longer so isolated and certainly not nearly so little. It remains to be seen, of course, which of these writers will follow in Sappho's footsteps in the sense of having a lasting and profound effect upon readers and writers of centuries to come. As for Sappho herself, her prophecy in fragment 147 V. about her own work has clearly come to pass: "I say that even later someone will remember us."

chapter ■
eight

The Critical Reception

And not unhallowed was the page
By winged Love inscribed, to assuage
The pangs of vain pursuit;
Love listening while the Lesbian Maid
With the finest touch of passion swayed
Her own Aeolian lute.

—Wordsworth, *Upon the Same Occasion*, 1819

FOR OVER 2,600 YEARS, scholars, writers, and the public have debated the status of Sappho. Alternately, a literary superstar, sexual avatar, and women's libber, she was also thought to be a poor imitator of male poets, a sexual predator and deviant, and an excuse to shut the women's movement down entirely. To discuss Sappho, whether in the context of literary reception or popular reception, one necessarily encounters discussions of gender and sexuality theory that reflect more on the mores of the time than the reality and the literature of Sappho, largely due to its fractured state. Hence, critical reception to Sappho might easily be called critical reception to sexuality in literature. In Greek times, little was made of the notion of sexuality. Instead of the set notions of homo and heterosexual, the Greeks worked with notions of dominant and submissive, based first on social class, then on sex. So, a female from a wealthy family would have considerably more social power than a male of the slave class, as a teacher would have greater power than his/her students, as in the case, perhaps, of both Sappho and Socrates. In her own time, Sappho appeared to have been celebrated by the public and by noted intellectuals, like Plato who referred to her as "the tenth muse." Her sexuality would probably not have been of particular note because it did not defy the dominant/submissive hierarchy (Andreadis, 1–14). Instead, it was her work that defied popular standards, as she was a woman of great accomplishment. In the ensuing generations, particularly with the advent of Christianity and religious scholars, her reputation began to change.

In the 3rd century B.C. Posidippus referred to her as a "sensualist" reducing the lyric and erotic content of the poems to something minor and titillating. Two centuries later, Roman poet Catullus deeply admired Sappho, mimicking her turn from the traditionally male poetry of state to the more introspective and individual lyric poetry. Early critiques of Sappho acknowledged her contributions in terms of form and meter as well as content. A particular advocate of her metric innovations, Horace referred to her as "mascula" (Reynolds, 72) which has been interpreted to mean alternately (sometimes simultaneously) that she had so mastered the form as to be comparable to men or to mean that she was a lover of women, a tribad. Seneca added to the emphasis on her sexual life and the destruction of Sappho's reputation with his joking letter wherein he muses over whether Sappho was a prostitute (Reynolds, 72).

Perhaps the most lasting attack on Sappho's reputation and myth came from the Roman poet Ovid, who chose to adopt the voice of the poet, and with that voice, write a letter to Phaon, a young male lover who, according to Ovid's recorded legend, rejected the aging, reformed homosexual poet. She became a figure of pathetic fun. However damaging Ovid's interpretation might have been, it also kept Sappho in the public eye as physical instances of Sappho's poems were becoming fewer and fewer, while Ovid was being widely translated. The repeated sacks of the great libraries of Constantinople left few copies intact (Reynolds, 81–3). Other scholars believe that radical Christians, with the support of the Pope Gregory VII, burned copies of her poetry because she was a woman of power, a writer of erotic content, and more specifically, of what might be called 'homosexual content' which the Church fathers believed might lead to the conception of fewer Christians as it was not a procreative form of love.

Medieval times were dark for Sappho as they were for education in general; however, Ovid's "Sappho to Phaon" kept the poet in the mind of medieval scholars. During that time, the *Suda*, an encyclopedia from the 10th century set forth the notion that Sappho was two different people, one an aristocrat, lyric poet, and the inventor of the plectrum (an early precursor to the guitar pick), and the other a lovesick lesbian lyre player who thew herself off a cliff. Still, despite the attitudes of the time, as in later centuries, women were working to keep Sappho as a literary icon and role model. Christine de Pisan (1363–1431) wrote *The Book of the City of Ladies*, which offered entries on notable women. De Pisan effusively praised Sappho as a writer of greater literary merit; however, she made no mention of the female erotic love at the center of many of the poems. It seems that to make her case, de Pisan believed that she needed to carefully expurgate that portion of the story, particularly as part of her thesis in establishing female equality was to assert that women were not sexual manipulators. Any mention of Sappho's eros might have defeated that claim in the eyes of a hostile audience.

By the 16th century, Sappho was back to being a revered intellectual figure. Raphael included her in his painting of *Parnassus at the Vatican* and Renaissance scholar Thomas More was spreading her legend via the printing press and editions of Catullus and Ovid. Like de Pisan, he chose to not acknowledge the sexual content and homoerotic love in the poems. In 1582, English playwright, John Lyly wrote a play in which Sappho was played in homage to Queen Elizabeth I. The play emphasized the witty smarts of the poet and by extension, the queen, thereby raising her reputation to that of the learned and wise lady. Poet John Donne, on the other hand, a reader of Greek, believed Sappho to be learned, witty and sexual (Reynolds, 86).

In the 17th century, the French became great champions of Sappho as they would be in later centuries as well. In 1670, the first French translation of her collected fragments was printed, this time under her own name rather than one of the Roman poets who wrote in her name. Longinus's *On the Sublime* became very popular, and with it, his translation of Fragment 31. At this point, it also became de rigeur to preface her work with a "life," based on a very few facts. Critic Joan de Jean asserts that French literature and the recovery of Sappho were synonymous, particularly as the French canon really began to define itself during Neoclassicism (DeJean, 12). She believes that the construction of Sappho to that point, was largely created by the French and as such, has many of the French mores of the time, particularly an interest in the sexuality of the author.

In England, in 1652, John Hall translated Longinus into English, popularizing as the French had, his version of Fragment 31. The Restoration in England was a rich landscape in which to ressurect the eros of Sappho, after the stark morality of Cromwell. She appeared in ballads as a fallen maid, seduced by her beau; in a play as a learned poet in a garret, and in the poetry of Katherine Phillips, a reputed lesbian, as an influence. Phillips found Sappho to be a role model both personally and professionally. Critic Harriette Andreadis discusses this in more detail in *Sappho in Early Modern England.*

Alternatively, critic William Walsh claimed that while Sappho might be as witty as a man, she had created "a new sort of sin" (Reynolds, 100) when she pursued erotic love with other women. The English made a polyglot of the poet; she was alternately, as per usual, the sexual deviant, fallen woman and the learned lady and poet. But she had also taken on a third role, as role model to women who identified as lesbians. Sappho's work and interest gave women a sense of their history lurking somewhere within the silence of society and academia. Someone, both talented and famous, had loved, learned and written before them.

As the next century began, poet Alexander Pope translated Ovid's "Sappho to Phaon" in 1707, and newspaper man, Joseph Addison published two articles on her life and work in *The Spectator*, bringing her to broad audiences. At the same time, Lady Mary Wortley Montague eloped with her lover to escape a forced marriage and began holding salons in London. Montague embraced Sappho as a literary mother and publicly associated herself with the poet. After a falling out with Montague, Pope began publishing nasty poems, linking Montague with Sappho and calling them both diseased and promiscuous. At this point, Sappho had become a thing of warning meant to keep women controlled and condemned. Male writers suggested that independence in women led to immoral lesbian behavior as in the case of Sappho.

Still, the public was not having the last word, critically, her reputation was improving. New translations of her work cropped up across Europe and a new intellectual trend was sweeping the continent: the sublime. Taken largely from Edmund Burke's *A Philosophical Enquiry into the Origins of our Ideas of the Sublime and the Beautiful*, published in 1757, and it re-introduced the ideas of the sublime (the awesome, the wild, the naturally powerful) versus the beautiful (the small, the pretty, the localized). Sappho's work, though lyric and personal, fell into the category of the sublime because of its conviction, myth making, and broad thinking. Of particular interest was her death leap, where she conceded to the awesome power of nature. Addison wrote of her in this context claiming that her story elicited both "terror and pity (Reynolds 150)." With Sappho's voice a part of the ongoing conversation regarding the sublime, women began to feel empowered. Again, Sappho had shown herself capable of the kind of higher thought that had once been thought the exclusive province of men.

Across the Channel, the French were worshipping Sappho, via the vehicle of Abbé Barthélemy's *Voyage du jeune Anacharsis en Gréce*, a book which led to eight more tales with voluminous notes. Under his influence, Germaine Necker, Baronne de Stael, wrote a series of novels, reimagining Sappho as a publicly beloved writer, who eventually dies of heartbreak, but not before she empowers her daughter with education. The character became an inspiration for women and writers of the 19th century, though they also led to her eventual exile due to her battles with Napoleon. Napoleon encouraged male writers and painters to stress worship of Phaon rather than Sappho. Phaon was the hero, and as such, de Stael became the villain as she embodied the Sappho figure. Her vilification was a convenient political ploy for Napoleon who eventually exiled her (Reynolds 172–4). The Marquis de Sade used Sappho as a leader of a fictive band of violent lesbians, and in 1857, Baudelaire published *Fleurs du Mal,* which contained three lesbian poems that harkened back to the destructive and decadent lesbians of de Sade; they also helped make the book one of the most controversial of the century.

In 1816, Friedrich Gottlieb Welcker published his now infamous treatise in which he claimed that Sappho was asexual and chaste, simply because the Greeks would not have supported something crude like tribadism. He further asserted that the use of female pronouns was a de facto norm for beauty, and thus not particular to any woman, leaving Sappho pure of any base desire. His argument lasted for a number of years. The 1850s were good years for Sappho. In Germany, Theodor Bergk made a definitive translation that lasted until the 20th century in terms of its authority and influence. Indeed, Henry Thorton Wharton took his English version from Bergk's Greek.

In England, Sappho fascinated a new group of writers: the Romantics. Popular attention was turning from the Classical and the Neo-classical back to the imagination and the sublime. With her emphasis on the perspective of the individual and the private felt moment, Sappho was adopted by Shelley and

Byron. Later, Tennyson wrote in a female voice like that of Sappho and was known to have studied her extensively. Of course, with his classical education, he could make sense of the conversation. Women of the time, for the most part, were not as lucky and the Sappho with which they were left was one based on mythologies recorded for the most part by men.

Pre-Raphaelite poet Charles Algernon Swinburne became a passionate advocate and devotee of Sappho's. He translated her poems and called her his muse and sister. He was not the only one claiming kinship. With the beginning of the first wave of feminism, women were gaining education, entering the exclusive worlds of Greek and Latin and for the first time were able to read the unadulterated texts of Sappho for themselves. Gone were the polite changes in pronouns put in the text by Jean-Francois Boissonade. Gone was the commentary on sexuality provided by scholars outlining the "life" of Sappho. Part of Sappho's appeal was in her being a part of the myth of the academy, from which women had been excluded for so long. Learning Greek and Latin would open the academy and its secrets to women. John Addington Symonds, an Oxford don, openly espoused education for women. He taught Greek and during that time, became friends with a lesbian couple, Katherine Bradley and Edith Cooper, who wrote together under the pseudonym, Michael Field. The two women linked education and freedom and reinterpreted the famous Wharton text in 1885. Symonds wrote about Sappho's metrics, returning her work to the primary focus of study, and William Cory taught Mary Coleridge who, in turn, wrote "Marriage" in Sapphic meter. Both men wrote about Sappho, and perhaps not coincidentally, both men were gay.

In 1895, another fragment, part of number 5, was unearthed in central Egypt. The find resulted in another wave of interest in Sappho. At the same time, Natalie Barney, an

American heiress, used Sappho as a figurehead for her salon of learned women, many of whom were lesbians. Poet Renée Vivien worked to encourage women to study Greek. She herself invoked both Sappho and the Sapphic lifestyle. She even returned to Lesbos on a pilgrimage to the poet's home. More and more, women were embracing Sappho as a proud and fruitful lesbian foremother. Still, her reputation as a lesbian was being contested by other scholars. In 1911, German scholar Ulrich von Wilamowitz-Mollendorf revived Friedrich Welcker's verson of her chastity, claiming that Sappho was a schoolteacher who protected the virtue of her students, which was why she was so often surrounded by women. The legacy of that reading has become fodder for twentieth century examination by Holt Parker.

Around the turn of the 20th century, archeology was also becoming legitimized within academia and with it, scholars were beginning to be able to piece together what society might have been like in Sappho's time. Just as the world was beginning to piece together the past, the present began to fracture. The world was at war, and the precise forms of the past no longer seemed to fit the broken present. Indeed, poets were coming up with new forms and new imperatives, particularly the Modernists and within that group, the Imagists, started by Ezra Pound. Like Sappho, Pound treasured concision and image. Sappho's influence can be seen in the work of a number of modernists, most notably perhaps, H.D. who used the fragments for inspiration and wrote a meditation on Sappho as well. Amy Lowell, Edna St. Vincent Millay, Virginia Woolf and others showed interest in the poet as well. Margaret Goldsmith wrote *Sappho of Lesbos: A Psychological Reconstruction of Her Life* (1938) based on the fragments as a cohesive narrative. Around the 1960s and '70s, Sappho was re-appropriated as a free wheeling swinger and a lesbian-feminist activist invoked in the books *Sappho was a Right-On Woman: A Liberated View of Les-bianism* as well as *Sappho: The Art of Loving Women.* Her name was also emblazoned across the cover of *Playboy* in the 1970s with glossy pictures of women loving women, but the end of the twentieth century brought her under the magnifying glass of literary critics, who examined her as a poet, a study in gender and sexuality studies, and a writer of lasting influence.

Critics took multiple perspectives, examining the poet in terms of her historical reception. In *Fictions of Sappho: 1546–1937,* Joan de Jean traces Sappho's entrance into the French literary tradition, asserting that the poet was a way for women to come into their own writing and literary talent and a way for men to "come of age" in writing by either speaking through the poet and saying something new about her life. De Jean links the creation of the French canon to the creation of various Sappho legends and myths, though she also considers those fictions created by other countries and adopted by the French. In *Victorian Sappho,* critic Yopie Prins does a similar, though more narrowly focused, study of Sappho in the writing of Victorian poets, arguing that Sappho helped to define the lyric as a feminine form. Prins furthers this project in examining sexual politics and its engendering of Victorian poetry, and by extension, portions of literary history. Critic Harriette Andreadis explores the presence of Sappho in early modern England. Her study examines the poet's influence on the gendering of the lyric and the articulation of homoeroticism between women. She views Sappho briefly as a specific figure, then devotes herself to the primary myths surrounding the writer and her legacy. Finally, scholar Ruth Vanita, in *Sappho and the Virgin Mary: Same Sex Love and the English Literary Imagination,* looks at the idea of "love between creators", that is the interplay between writers and literary ancestors, particularly woman to woman, and its celebratory nature. In what Vanita calls the "Sapphic model" she asserts that the model "develops a passionate dialogue between women as a paradigm for lyric intensity and sublimity" (Vanita, 2). With the reconsideration of genre that this necessarily entails, she traces that through three primary literary periods, Romanticism, Aestheticism, and Bloomsbury.

Critic Jane McIntosh Snyder examines the world of Sappho, which is at its heart, a world of women, as the two genders were firmly segregated in their duties and roles in her study, *Lesbian Desire in the Lyrics of Sappho*. Looking at Sappho as a writer of relationships between women, suggests first that relationships

Alienation in the Classroom

In Ellen Louise Hart's article, "Literacy and the Lesbian/Gay Learner, " she cites a Classroom Climate Survey conducted by the Associated Students of the University of California, at Berkeley in 1984, in which gay and lesbian students "were the most uncomfortable in class, more than any other ethnic minority group, women, or the disabled" (Garnes et al., 122). The same study found that "82% of lesbian and gay students surveyed had been subjected to pejorative stereotypical comments about homosexuals by instructors." Though Hart is leery of comparing suffering, she does note that the survey confirms, at least, the suffering felt by students in the classroom, and the silence that may result. As with the pronoun games employed by translators to make Sappho heterosexual or at the very least, not homosexual, students censor themselves to hide their homosexuality in the classroom environment. Hart contends that the fear of exposure hurts student writing as they are crippled by their inability to be specific about their feelings and lives which leads to generalizations and vague examples. This in turn leads not only to poor grades, but to alienation and a feeling of having a lost identity.

between women, whether erotic or emotional, are worthy of study and second, that they are present in the poems. How do the poems change when they are examined through a woman-centered lens rather than a patriarchal, heterosexual lens? Snyder herself acknowledges that she is creating another fiction of Sappho; however, she takes her story primarily from the fragments and archeological and classical renderings of the times. Scholar Bernadette J. Brooten investigates early Christian responses to female homoeroticism, particularly as a force which made erotic contact between women suspect and heretical in her book, *Love Between Women.* She provides ample historical cultural context in which to view a wide variety of sexual designations assigned in the ancient world, well-beyond the traditional homo/heterosexual. She uses Sappho to set up a scaffolding for viewing female homoeroticism and female intellectual life in both the Roman and Byzantine periods. Poet and scholar Judy Grahn continues the work that she began in *Another Mother Tongue—Gay Words, Gay Worlds* in *The Highest Apple,* where she again focuses on Gay culture, this time with an emphasis on lesbian culture and the central place that poets, particularly Sappho have within it. She traces Sappho as a literary and cultural antecedent.

In *Sappho is Burning,* critic Page duBois discusses the difficulties in constructing a consistent narrative for Sappho, and the pleasures and necessity for examining the fractured pieces, rather than pressing towards a whole. DuBois engages the notion of the body of Sappho, both as a representation of desire and work(s). Scholar Lyn Hatherly Wilson also examines the creation of the Sappho narratives paying particular attention to the varied representations of gender between male and female writers and in their work.

Critic Margaret Reynolds traces 2,600 years of critical reception in *The Sappho Companion.* She augments her commentary on the historical and political factors influencing the poet's reception with excerpts from particularly famous work on or about the author. In addition, she wrote *The Sappho History* and it too traces critical reception but it looks closely at the question of audience and discussing the ways in which the perception of Sappho revealed more about the audience than the poet.

Finally, scholar Ellen Greene edited two collections of essays on Sappho, (*Reading Sappho: Contemporary Approaches* and *Re-Reading Sappho: Reception and Transition*) reflecting the major schools of thought in late 20th to early 21st century response to the writer. Scholars looked primarily at socio-cultural-historical reception, issues in translation, context in the oral tradition and the western canon, and gender and sexuality within the poems, their reception and their legacy.

In many ways, little has changed in terms of scholarly approach. Critics are still analyzing both the poet and the poems; they are still considering Sappho's legacy in terms of the needs and social mores of the time. Certainly, much has changed in gender and sexuality studies and that change has affected the current narrative of Sappho, but she remains, ultimately, an untouchable and unknowable figure, reworked to a tensile strength by the power of collective imagination and social need.

afterword

Thee, the storm-bird, nightingale-souled,
Brother of Sappho, the seas reclaim!
Age upon age have the great waves rolled
Mad with her music, exultant, aflame;
　　　　—Alfred Noyes "In Memory of Swinburne"

AFTER A MILLENIUM OF BEING STUDIED, Sappho's legacy is multi-faceted, both for culture and literature. As a writer, Sappho broke poetry from the language of the public moment and comment to the more intimate lyric, exploring the personal, the individually felt. Combined with her emphasis on eros, Sappho earned her designation of "the Poetess" as Homer was called "the Poet." Similarly, she made famous a stanzic structure that was later named for her. In these ways, among many others, she has affected poets across generations: the Romantics, the Modernists, the Greek comedians. Byron, Swindburne, Tennyson, H.D., Carolyn Kizer, Aphra Behn, Ovid, Longinus, Seneca, Hardy, Elizabeth Barrett Browning, Keats, Baudelaire, Anne Carson, Shelley, and Virginia Woolf all claim Sappho as literary kin. Even today, when Rae Dalven published an anthology of contemporary Greek women poets, she entitled it, *Daughters of Sappho.*

Additionally, because her poems were lyrics, she has inspired musicians across the centuries as well. Her poems lend themselves to music, suggesting the way in which they were originally appreciated. Because of the fragmented nature and the sense of melancholy and lost love within the poems, they translated easily into music. Composers, like writers, found that they could work in the space between the fragments to create something new, particularly in the opera. Gounod, Massenet, Pacini, Bree, Kanne, Reicha, Lissenko, and Schwartzendorf all embraced Sappho as a character ripe for representation. Orff and Brahms, among others, have written based on her work. Visual artists also embraced the writer, particularly during the Neo-classical movement. Her visage has been used to represent learned women and licentious women alike.

Still, for many, her legacy remains largely tied to her gender and her sexuality. Often used to represent female licentiousness, Sappho still invokes an image of people leering at lesbian lovers. Any internet search with her name will still turn up dozens of sites of lesbian pornography. Simultaneously, throughout the centuries, from Madame de Stael to the New Women of the twentieth century, Sappho represents one of the oldest figures in women's intellectual history. Women beginning in the 14th century cited Sappho as an example of male/female equality. Writers like Aphra Behn and intellectuals like Oxford don John Addington Symonds studied the poet and her work. Even today, college students study the writer, even independent groups outside of the Academy try to study and perpetuate the legacy. In California, a group of volunteer professional women have created the Sappho Project, dedicated to educating people about the work and life of the poet (*www.lesbian.org/sappho-project/*).

As a corollary, Sappho also became a leading figure in gay and lesbian rights. Only through education could one become as empowered as the famous Sappho, and only through education could one even become aware of such a woman. Many women, then as now, believed that with education came freedom, and with freedom, sexual rights, and Sappho represented all of those things.

As a woman writing about erotic love between women, Sappho opened up a huge space for lesbian writers and intellectuals. Poet and writer Collette and Natalie Barney embraced Sappho as a lesbian heroine in Paris in the 1800s and Sidney Abbott titled her book of 1972, *Sappho Was a Right-on Woman: a Liberated View of Lesbianism*. Today, her name is attached to dozens of groups supporting lesbian women across the world, from Euro-Sappho to Canada's 11th annual "Wilde About Sappho," Ottawa's annual celebration of gay and lesbian literature. Importantly, she remains connected to literature by lesbian women, making one of her strongest contributions that of giving a traditionally silenced group a voice. Sappho spoke into a vast silence about the erotic lives of lesbian women. Only because there was Sappho could there be Adrienne Rich's *Twenty-One Love Poems*. Ultimately, the poet's legacy will be told and retold through the centuries as notions about sexuality and gender relations change; however, to date, an astonishing number of social causes, poems, music, and art can be directly attributed to her influence.

NOTE: The fragments of Sappho's poetry are cited throughout this book according to the numbering system used in Eva-Maria Voigt, ed., *Sappho et Alcaeus: Fragmenta* (Amsterdam: Athenaeum-Polak & Van Gennep, 1971).

Andreadis, Harriette. *Sappho in Early Modern England: Female Same-Sex Literary Erotics 1550–1714.* Chicago: University of Chicago Press, 2001.

Brooten, Bernadette J. *Love Between Women.* Chicago: University of Chicago Press, 1996.

Dalven, Rae, ed. and trans. *Daughters of Sappho: Contemporary Greek Women Poets.* Cranbury, NJ: Associated University Presses, 1994.

DeJean, Joan. *Fictions of Sappho, 1546–1937.* Chicago: University of Chicago Press, 1989.

Hart, Ellen Louise. "Literacy and the Gay and Lesbian Learner." *Writing Lives. Garnes,* Sara, David Humphries, Vic Mortimer, Jennifer Phegley, Kathleen R. Wallace, ed. Boston: St. Martin's Press, 1996.

Leaska, Mitchell. *Granite and Rainbow: The Hidden Life of Virginia Woolf.* Farrar, Strauss, Giroux: New York, 1998.

Reynolds, Margaret, ed. *The Sappho Companion.* London: Chatto & Windus, 2000.

Voigt, Eva-Maria, ed., *Sappho et Alcaeus: Fragmenta.* Amsterdam: Athenaeum-Polak & Van Gennep, 1971.

Burnett, Anne Pippin. *Three Archaic Poets: Archilochus, Alcaeus, Sappho.* Cambridge: Harvard University Press, 1983.

DuBois, Page. *Sappho is Burning.* Chicago: The University Chicago Press, 1995.

Greene, Ellen, ed. *Reading Sappho: Contemporary Approaches.* Berkeley; University of California Press, 1996.

————, ed. *Re-Reading Sappho: Reception and Transmission.* Berkeley; University of California Press, 1996.

Jenkyns, Richard. *Three Classical Poets: Sappho, Catullus, and Juvenal.* London: Duckworth, 1982.

Mulroy, David, ed. *Early Greek Lyric Poetry.* Ann Arbor: University of Michigan Press, 1992.

Page, Denys. *Sappho and Alcaeus: An Introduction to the Study of Ancient Lesbian Poetry.* Oxford: Oxford University Press, 1955.

Pomeroy, Sarah B. *Goddesses, Whores, Wives, and Slaves: Women in Classical Antiquity.* New York: Schocken, 1975.

Reynolds, Margaret. *The Sappho History.* New York: Palgrave Macmillan, 2003.

Sappho. In *Greek Lyric.* David A. Campbell, trans. Loeb Classical Library. Cambridge: Harvard University Press, 1982.

————. *Sappho: A Garland.* Jim Powell, trans. New York: Farrar, Straus, Giroux, 1993.

————. *Sappho's Lyre: Archaic Lyric and Women Poets of Ancient Greece.* Diane J. Rayor, trans. Berkeley: University of California Press, 1991.

Snyder, Jane McIntosh. *The Woman and the Lyre: Women Writers in Classical Greece and Rome.* Carbondale: Southern Illinois University Press, 1989.

————. *Lesbian Desire in the Lyrics of Sappho.* New York: Columbia University Press, 1997.

Vanita, Ruth. *Sappho and the Virgin Mary: Same-sex Love and the English Literary Imagination.* New York: Columbia University Press, 1996.

Wilson, Lyn Hatherly. *Sappho's Sweetbitter Songs: Configurations of Female and Male in Ancient Greek Lyric.* New York: Routledge, 1996.

Winkler, John J. *The Constraints of Desire: The Anthropology of Sex and Gender in Ancient Greece.* New York: Routledge, 1990.

WEBSITES

The Divine Sappho
classicpersuasion.org/pw/sappho/index.htm

glbtq: literature: Sappho
www.glbtq.com/literature/sappho.html

The Poems of Sappho: Index
www.sacred-texts.com/cla/sappho/

Sappho
home.infionline.net/~ddisse/sappho.html

Wikipedia
en.wikipedia.org/wiki/Sappho

WORKS BY AND ABOUT MODERN WOMEN POETS INFLUENCED BY SAPPHO

Bloom, Harold, ed. *H.D.* New York: Chelsea House, 2002.

Broumas, Olga. *Beginning with O.* New Haven: Yale University Press, 1977.

Doolittle, Hilda. *Collected Poems, 1912–1944.* Louis L. Martz, ed. New York: New Directions, 1983.

———. *Notes on Thought and Vision and The Wise Sappho.* San Francisco: City Lights Books, 1982.

Evans, Elizabeth. *May Sarton, Revisited,* Boston: Twayne Publishers, 1989.

Gould, Jean. *Amy: The World of Amy Lowell and the Imagist Movement.* New York: Dodd, Mead, 1975.

Heymann, C. David. *American Aristocracy: The Lives and Times of James Russell, Amy, and Robert Lowell.* New York: Dodd, Mead, 1980.

Hunting, Constance, ed. *May Sarton: Woman and Poet.* Orono, Maine: National Poetry Foundation, 1982.

Jay, Karla. *The Amazon and the Page. Natalie Clifford Barney and Renée Vivien.* Bloomington: Indiana University Press, 1988.

Lowell, Amy. *Complete Poetical Works.* Boston: Houghton Mifflin, 1955.

Middlebrook, Diane Wood, and Marilyn Yalom, ed. *Coming to Light: American Women Poets in the Twentieth Century.* Ann Arbor: University of Michigan Press, 1985.

Robinson, Janice S. *H.D., The Life and Work of an American Poet.* Boston: Houghton Mifflin, 1982.

Sarton, May. *May Sarton: A Self-Portrait.* Marita Simpson and Martha Wheelock, ed. New York: W.W. Norton, 1982.

———. *Selected Poems of May Sarton.* Serena Sue Hilsinger and Lois Brynes, ed. New York: Norton, 1978.

Vivien, Renée. *At the Sweet Hour of Hand in Hand.* Sandia Belgrade, trans. Weatherby Lake, Mo.: Naiad Press, 1979.

———. *A Woman Appeared to Me.* Jeannette H. Foster, trans., with an introduction by Gayle Rubin. Reno, Nev.: Naiad Press, 1976.

INDEX

Abbott, Sidney, 112
Absence and desire theme, 55,
56–58, 96
"Absence" (Lowell), 82
Alcaeus, 5, 13, 31
Aldington, Richard, 86
Alexandria edition of Sappho's
work, 61–62
American Academy of Arts and
Letters Award of Merit for
poetry, 86
Anaktoria (the most beautiful thing
on earth), 50–53
Ancient Greece
androcentric information from,
22–24
dominant and submissive vs.
homo or hetero, 104
dramas and epics, 24
erotic relationships in, 6–8
festivals, 27–28, 31
gift giving among lovers, 29, 40
Hellenistic period, 61
Lesbos and, 4–6, 30–32
literary patterns, 50
political structure, 22
pottery of, 23, 29, 34
prayer pattern, 37–39
view of Aphrodite, 41
women/girls, upper-class, 25–29
women's status, 23–24
Andreadis, Harriette, 107, 112
Andromache and Hector, 64–66
*Another Mother Tongue—Gay
Words, Gay Worlds* (Grahn),
114
Antipater of Thessaloniki, 17
Aphrodite. *See also* "Hymn to
Aphrodite"
in early Greek literature, 41
Phaon and, 14
prayer to, for safety of Charaxus,
68–69
Sappho's invitation to, 42–44

Sappho's relationship with,
40–41, 44
Sarton's poem to, 94
Apple grove song, 42–44
Archaeological research, 5, 63
Arion, 4
Aristophanes, 24
Artemis, 89–90
"Artemis" (Broumas), 98
Aspasia of Miletus, 29
Atthis (the woman who has gone
away to Lydia), 53–56

Barbitos (seven-stringed lyre), 37
Barney, Natalie, 83–84, 110–11
Barthélemy, Abbé, 108–9
Baudelaire, Charles, 109
The beautiful vs. the sublime, 108
Beauty, songs about, 70–71
Bergk, Theodor, 109
Biography vs. legend, 11
"Birthday on the Acropolis"
(Sarton), 93–94
"Bitterness" (Broumas), 97
The Book of the City of Ladies (de
Pisan), 106
Bradley, Katherine, 110
Broken tongue (Fragment 31 V),
46–50, 106–7
Brooten, Bernadette, 36, 114
Broumas, Olga, 96–101
Brown, Rita Mae, xiii
Burke, Edmund, 108
Byron, Lord, 45

Cather, Willa, 75
Catullus, 17, 46, 104
Charaxus (brother), 68–69
Childbearing in ancient Greece, 26
Christianity, 17, 114
Classroom Climate Survey (1984),
113
Coleridge, Mary, 110

124

CONTRIBUTORS

JANE MCINTOSH SNYDER is Professor Emeritus, Ohio State University and a professional violinist. Her books include *Lesbian Desire in the Lyrics of Sappho* and *The Woman and the Lyre: Women Writers in Classical Grece and Rome.*

CAMILLE-YVETTE WELSCH is a lecturer in English and the Advising Coordinator in English and American Studies for the Pennsylvania State University. Her reviews and poetry have appeared in *Barrow Street, The Women's Review of Books, Calyx, and Foreword Magazine.*

LESLÉA NEWMAN is the author of 50 books including the picture books *Heather Has Two Mommies* and *The Boy Who Cried Fabulous;* the short story collections *A Letter to Harvey Milk* and *Out of the Closet and Nothing to Wear;* the poetry collection *Still Life with Buddy;* the novels In *Every Laugh a Tear* and *Jailbait;* and the writing manual, *Write from the Heart.* She has received many literary awards including Poetry Fellowships from the Massachusetts Artists Fellowship Foundation and the National Endowment for the Arts, the Highlights for Children Fiction Writing Award, the James Baldwin Award for Cultural Achievement, and three Pushcart Prize Nominations. Nine of her books have been Lambda Literary Award finalists.